The Ornamental Vegetable Garden

Diana Anthony

Photographs by Gil Hanly

W

Warwick Publishing

Toronto   Los Angeles

For the non-gardening husband and my daughter Sarah.
To both with love.

Front cover: Liz Mackmurdie's country potager, see page 15.
Back cover: The small-space potager of Annie Heywood, see page 95.
Page 1 (half title): Rosemary Verey's famous modern potager at
Barnsley House, England.
Page 2: The author's own small potager illustrates how well flowers
and vegetables may be mixed in an informal manner to give produce
with pleasure.
Page 3 (title page): The versatility of herbs and vegetables makes them
excellent container specimens in situations where space is scarce.

635
A628
(.1

Published in the United States and Canada by Warwick Publishing Inc.
388 King Street West #111, Toronto, Ontario M5V 1K2
1300 North Alexandria Avenue, Los Angeles, California 90027

Distributed in the United States and Canada by Firefly Books Ltd.
3680 Victoria Park Avenue, Willowdale, Ontario M2H 3K1

First published in New Zealand in 1997 by David Bateman Ltd.
30 Tarndale Grove, Albany, Auckland

© text Diana Anthony, 1998
© photographs Gil Hanly, 1998
© David Bateman Ltd., 1998

Design by Errol McLeary
Typesetting by TTS Jazz
Printed in China by Colorcraft Ltd

CONTENTS

INTRODUCTION
The concept and history of the potager

Gardens are always evocative. My passion for edible gardening was nurtured in childhood when a well stocked plot of vegetables was as important to my family as fresh air and sunlight. They were firm believers in the old adage 'one for the birds, one for the bugs, and one for me', and all produce was grown in good home-made compost without recourse to toxic sprays or chemical fertilisers. I can still smell the rich chocolate earth emeralded with foliage, frothed with creamy cauliflowers, jewelled with balls of ruby beet, and with the purple-black globes of

Opposite: Potagers were laid out many centuries ago in elaborately formal parterres and knot gardens. Although the same principles have been applied in the basic design of this grander potager, the diversity and informality of the plantings give the garden at the Old Rectory, Northampton, a pleasantly relaxed ambience.
Above: Raised beds of bold geometric shapes offer strong design concepts in this unusual potager.

aubergines/eggplants. I can still taste young peas, scarlet sun-warmed tomatoes and soft fruits picked and eaten straight from the plant. I remember the magic (still undiminished half a century later!) of excavating the soil and finding tiny new golden-skinned potatoes.

A particular joy was to accompany my grandparents into their vegetable garden, carrying in my small hands their huge 'picking basket'. I was allowed to choose and harvest whichever edibles took my fancy, the only rule being that I ate everything I picked – I can think of no better way to make a small child eat its greens!

Highly productive though these gardens were, the growing of food was strictly a utilitarian process, all vegetables marching in rigid soldier-straight ranks and rows across a plot discreetly tucked away at the bottom of the back yard. It wasn't until many years later, living in England and in European countries such as France, Switzerland and Austria that I found edible gardens where fragrant herbs and flowers were folded in with the fruit and vegetables – as in medieval gardens of long ago.

Here, houses large and small rejoice in immaculately maintained, lovingly tended potager gardens, often at the front of the house. (The word 'potager' is derived from the French word *potage*, which does not mean pots and pans but a thick vegetable soup generously flavoured with herbs.) The pathway to the front door is a delicious assault on the senses – flanked by clumps of bee-embroidered crops, made fragrant by pungent sun-released oils from culinary herbs, and colourful with flowers grown as companion plants or simply for picking for the house.

Gardens such as these, where aesthetics and practicality are combined to create potagers which please both the gourmet gardener's palate and the creative gardener's palette, shaped the design of my subsequent edible gardens and led me to a study of the history of the ornamental vegetable garden and the writing of this book. A pleasure I wish to share with all gardeners.

This custom of growing vegetables, fruit, herbs and flowers in both an ornamental and utilitarian manner evolved in the monastery gardens and castle courtyards of medieval England and Europe. These modest plots were succeeded by the great gardens of wealthy landowners, and design for the foodstuff garden was subject to the same degree of formality and aesthetics as the rest of the garden.

Travellers returning to Europe from the Americas in the sixteenth century brought with them exotic edible plants treasured for both their beauty and their culinary value. They brought back vegetables such as potatoes, tomatoes, aubergines/eggplants, 'French' beans and pumpkins, and arranged them in formal patterns in parterres which was the prevailing style of gardening at this time. The beds themselves were strictly geometric in shape and often bordered by low hedges of clipped box (*Buxus sempervirens*),

or by evergreen herbs such as lavender, rosemary or santolina (*S. chamaecyparissus*). Sometimes several different types of hedging were used to create the effect of interweaving colours and textures, and the fashion was for knot gardens or parterres of complicated design.

The plants and herbs were chosen not only for their food value but for their contrasting colours, size, leaf shape and texture, and carefully grouped accordingly to give maximum visual effect. The arrangement of the traditional potager was strictly symmetrical, and within the linear confines of its hedges and old brick paths, wicker support frames, twiggy tepees, trellises, fruit tunnels, topiary, espalier frames and arbours all combined to create an attractive setting for edible plants.

The most elaborate potager in medieval times was the Potager du Roi at Versailles which was created for the 'Sun King', Louis XIV, by landscape gardener Jean-Baptiste de la Quintinie in 1683. The gardens have been maintained ever since as the most famous edible garden in the world. La Quintinie developed the fruit pruning systems which we still use today, and examples of many shapes and forms are still maintained at Versailles.

Internationally acclaimed potager gardens of a more modern vintage are those of the Château de Villandry near Tours in France. Laid out around 1906 when the property was restored by Dr Joachim Carvallo, the kitchen garden covers 0.4 hectares (1 acre) divided into nine separate squares. These in turn are each divided into a highly individual pattern of edible and floral plantings.

The most famous of modern potager gardens, created by well known British gardener and writer Rosemary Verey, is situated at Barnsley House in Gloucestershire in England. In addition to featuring rare edibles and innovative planting combinations, special features include an arbour covered with golden hops, and a tunnel which supports marrows flanked by giant sunflowers. Sweet peas and edible peas, some with two-tone lilac flowers, are trained up bamboo poles set diagonally across two small square beds in a cross pattern. Fruit trees are trained into espaliers and cordons of diverse forms.

These grand potagers are a living reminder that growing food need not always be a strictly utilitarian business. Although our present-day gardens are far removed from the grounds of French châteaux or country estates, modern potagers such as Barnsley House show that the art of providing the household with an abundance of fruit, vegetables, herbs and flowers in a setting that is as attractive to the eye as the rest of the garden is enjoying an unprecedented revival.

Why plant a potager?

It is my hope that this book will illustrate that the ornamental kitchen garden presents every creative gardener with an exciting challenge, that the end product – produce with pleasure – brings the bonus of home-grown foodstuffs which, organically raised, have not been subjected to toxic sprays during growth. The tired, cling-film asphyxiated salad stuffs and vegetables bought from the supermarket bear no resemblance to the fresh crunchy produce harvested from one's own garden.

Home-grown vegetables literally reacquaint one's taste buds with the true flavour of an edible plant, and in addition, the 'grow your own' philosophy brings with it the distinct advantage of economy on the home front.

The traditional old fashioned stalwart vegetables are still happily here, but seedsmen's catalogues worldwide also offer them in modern hybrid forms with fruit and foliage of exciting colours and textures. The potagist has at his or her disposal a huge range of edibles of international origin – wonderful leafy vegetables from the Orient (particularly popular with those who enjoy Thai cuisine, and dishes from other Asian countries), fabulous salad plants, 'baby' gourmet vegetables and dwarf fruit trees some-

times bearing not one strain of fruit but two.

Vegetable foliage form, colour and texture is extremely diverse and will combine to form planting arrangements with enormous visual appeal – further enhanced by the low borders of evergreen hedges or shrubby herbs. In addition, the more formal design of the classic potager is well suited to the smaller gardens of today, and seedsmen are concentrating more and more on mini edible vegetables which will grow well in small gardens and containers.

The symmetrical confines of the modern potager is pleasing to the eye and maximises every centimetre of soil within. Many vegetables such as beans and peas may be grown vertically on tepees, archways or frames, leaving valuable ground space free for crops of more terrestrial growth habits. Even marrows, squash or courgettes/zucchini become focal points when suspended from an arch rather than hidden beneath foliage on the ground.

Soft fruit bushes may be trained as standards, vines and fruit trees espaliered along walls or frames, fulfilling the dual role of pleasing design and providing maximum produce in minimum space. Conifers or box hedging plants clipped as topiary specimens, standardised lavender, rosemary, or miniature roses look delightful combined with herbs and vegetables and enhance the pleasing symmetry of traditional potager design.

The vegetable garden of today is an exciting place where art and practicality have married; their offspring – a fabulous range of 'designer veg' which are easy to grow, visually pleasing, and exceptionally good to eat!

CHAPTER ONE

PLANNING AND DESIGN

The 'ground rules' advocated by Louis XIV's gardener, La Quintinie, as the basic practical requirements for a good potager are as relevant today as they were in medieval times.

The ground chosen must be good whatever the Colour be and have a good convenience to water, the site should be set upon a small rising of which the weather situation must be favourable, design should be of an agreeable figure and all should be enclos'd with reasonably high walls, the access easy and convenient.

Art of French Vegetable Gardening, Louisa Jones (full details in bibliography)

Opposite: The design of this developing potager illustrates how dynamic the use of geometric shape can be in garden landscaping, and how a formal design may still be created in an awkward or irregular space.
Above: Although this is a potager in the grand style, its basic design elements would adapt well to smaller scale home vegetable gardens.

This famous gardener of long ago knew the value of providing a sheltered, sunny and free-draining site for the cultivation of edibles. Walls and hedges were designed to protect the garden from harsh winds, and to create a favoured micro-climate which would lead to extended growing periods.

Choosing the site

When choosing a site for a potager, it is important to keep in mind not only the vagaries of the weather but the geography and ambience of the garden as a whole. Will the potager be on show to visitors, and from what other vantage points in the garden will it be visible? Will it be in clear view from the house windows or terrace, in which case it may be seen from above as a beautifully laid-out tapestry. Will it be presented as a main feature bordered only by dwarf hedges – in which case it will be open and dramatically displayed – or will it be concealed, walled and secret so that one comes upon it suddenly as a hidden treasure?

Viewpoints and perspective

If your potager's design has a fairly simple geometric layout, it will be easily seen from many viewpoints, which illustrates the need for it to look pleasing from all angles. One ill-placed block of slow-growing broccoli, for example, will hide or detract from smaller more colourful plants near or behind it for the whole season. If the potager is too large to be admired from one place, you will need to arrange a series of viewing points. This rule also applies if you want to grow a large variety of edible plants. Too many different varieties, even in one big picture, can create a messy overall view, so it is wiser to create a series of smaller pictures within the one large frame. With judicious planning you can place frames of espaliered fruit or vines, topiary specimens, hedges or screens to create a series of small garden rooms. This also adds a pleasant feeling of intimacy and surprise to the general ambience of the garden, making the observer wonder what is in the next area.

The natural places to pause in any garden are just inside the entrance, at the corners, the centre and at the junction of paths. People will also pause automatically at seats and even if they do not sit, they will stand here for a few moments to gaze at the garden as a whole. How well did you plan the planting of your garden? A good test is to walk immediately to all these places in your potager and see if they are pleasing or less than pleasing to the eye.

If you have had to create your garden from an awkward shape and have not been able to arrange the beds with the symmetry they need, the answer (as with any less than desirable feature) is to make a focal point of any problem areas instead. Plan for a really eyecatching crop to screen the difficult patch – a stand of tall sunflowers, a tepee of unusual runner beans, handsome clusters of fruit, beautiful or unusual

vegetables, or crops imaginatively displayed – cucurbits suspended overhead, for example, instead of hidden beneath leaves on the ground. Plantings such as these will halt the feet and unattractive areas will be less obvious.

There are a number of other ways visitors might be encouraged to pause at favoured viewpoints or gaze in a particular direction. A central focal point such as a sun dial, a circular bed, or a handsome topiary specimen in a container will cause their feet to stray from a straight pathway. A short tunnel or archway framing an enticing glimpse of the garden invites immediate exploration. The same is true of any corner – the eyes and the feet are drawn around the curve to discover what lies around the bend.

In an area where there are block plantings of low-growing crops, the contrast of vertical accents or a background framework may be provided with plantings of tall plants such as globe or Jerusalem artichokes, sweetcorn, burgundy-coloured amaranths, broad beans with scented black and white flowers, or sweet peas scrambling up a frame. The basic rule with focal points is that they should be in proportion to the scale of their surroundings. If the focal point is to draw the eye to the end of a long axis, it will need to be large – a 2 m (7 ft) silvery cardoon in all its thistle-like glory, for example – or it will fade into the background. However, if it is to draw the eye to the centre point of a medium-sized potager, the same cardoon will be handsome but threatening! A single standard lavender or rosemary bush would be a much safer option in this position.

Suggestions for plantings with visual impact for lower punctuation marks might include a stand of red or gold rainbow chard, a block planting of golden courgettes/zucchini, or pumpkins of orange-red tangled through with dwarf nasturtiums of similar tonings. The planting permutations for visual excitement in the potager are endless. Unlike 'hard' focal points such as statuary, plants change throughout their growth so that visual interest is

Above: This traditional potager of strong classical design features immaculately clipped dwarf hedges, enhancing the softer forms and colours of the vegetable foliage, particularly that of the fern-like carrot fronds in the foreground. A climbing bean in a terracotta pot makes a pleasing centrepiece and the fruit trees espaliered on Cotswold stone walls are underplanted with marrows and zucchinis.

Left: This potager is in the early stages of development and its basic design and layout can be clearly seen. Geometrically precise beds are neatly edged with timber and the L-shaped beds which mitre the corners are useful for plantings of soft fruit bushes, citrus or herbs. Although the basic ground plan is formal, the potager is enclosed with informal plantings of fruit trees, lavender and a curving box hedge. To the right, a stout trellis frame for the support of climbing crops or espaliered fruit creates a strong design feature.

Left: Although the design layout of this highly productive potager is basically formal, a sleepy scarecrow and luxuriant plantings of mixed flowers and vegetables impart a sense of fun. The apothecary's rose, *R. gallica officinalis*, underplanted with box makes an attractive focal point at centre.

Right: This newly developing potager features bold design concepts, interesting bed edgings and traditional fences and archways of woven willow prunings. The latter provide support for climbing beans later in the season. The handsome bay tree in the terracotta pot is underplanted with herbs and edged with santolina.

constantly maintained. Take care, however, not to make too many dramatic statements – they will cancel each other out, or the overall effect will be overwhelming. The eye will be as effectively drawn to a favoured area by a well planned juxtaposition of bed shapes and the directions of rows within the beds.

Irregular or awkward-shaped sites

If the only area you have available in which to create a potager is an awkward shape, it need not prevent you from making a symmetrical pattern. You can do much with the planning of plantings and the shape of your beds to balance the picture. With a little careful thought, especially round the edges of the plot, it will be possible to use all available cropping space without compromising the shape of your main pattern.

You can alter squares and rectangles to rhomboids, adjust the length of L-shapes, or squash circles slightly on one side. This juggling will still allow you to fit them into awkward spots while still aligning with your central axis. If possible, it is better to adjust the shape of the larger beds without it being obvious that you have done so. Employ a little native cunning by making the adjustment look like a deliberate manoeuvre rather than a mistake. Place vertical accent plants or structures strategically to distract the eye if you have had to bend a path that should be straight, or employ planted containers so that no one can stand at a viewpoint which shows uneven sides or angles.

Steep sites

I am often asked if it is possible to create a potager if the only space available is on a steep sloping site. This is entirely possible since

This 'under construction' potager illustrates the challenging design principles required for establishing a garden on a steep site. The slope has been cut into terraces and raised beds shaped into the hillside have been formed from built-up layers of weathered railway sleepers.

spatial definition and symmetry can be achieved just as well by a change of level as by a pattern of beds on a flat site. The potager may be designed as a series of simple terraces, remembering the basic rule that the steeper the slope, the narrower the step. A drop of 45 cm (18 in) over 9 m (30 ft) can be converted to 3 m (10 ft) wide areas with three wooden barriers 15–20 cm (6–7 in) high, as long as these barriers are attached to stout stakes driven in at least 60 cm (2 ft) deep. Provided there is a good depth of soil overall, there will be no restriction on what may be grown. It is not advisable to have a path at the top edge of each step, as walking too close to the edge may burst the barriers.

A terraced potager has several advantages: from above the whole of the pattern makes an attractive tapestry; from ground level you do not have to bend quite so far to pick plants on

Above: Neatly clipped hedges of box and sculptured topiary specimens combine to provide strong form and to create parterres of a more formal design in this larger potager. The brick pathway laid in a simple design draws the eye to a traditional wooden archway.

Below: It is not always possible to choose the ideal site for one's garden, and overcoming the design challenges presented by a long narrow section is a common problem. The owner of this site has created the illusion of width by breaking it up into four individual beds and by not compromising on the generous six-brick span of the pathway which gives an added feeling of breadth. The width of the beds is further maximised by plantings moving from low at the front to taller at the back.

the edge of each step; and you can utilise the step edge to grow plants such as strawberries or dwarf beans which would otherwise need support to prevent their fruit trailing on the ground.

If you absolutely have to have a perfect geometric shape to work with and feel there is one awkward area in the overall design that cannot be disguised, the solution is a tall hedge or fence to screen it off. The space need not be lost since it will still be invaluable for compost bins, stakes, toolshed, or all the other less attractive paraphernalia of vegetable gardening.

Long narrow sites

A common problem in the smaller rear gardens of modern homes is that the site for a vegetable garden is long and narrow. Long narrow beds aligned down a narrow garden make it look even narrower, and the perspective lines need to be adjusted. There are a number of ways in which a long narrow potager can be given the illusion of width.

1. Plant rows of vegetables in solid blocks across the beds rather than lengthways.
2. Create triangular beds with the apices pointing towards the entrance to the potager to create a broadening effect.
3. Progressively larger plants planted from front to back will reduce the impression of distance, just as the opposite progression will make a short garden appear longer.
4. Plan block plantings of taller plants with substantial body at the furthest point of the garden, or incorporate a strong focal point such as an archway, an espalier of fruit, a bold piece of statuary, clumps of soft-fruit bushes, tepees with climbing edibles, or any aspect offering a solid mass. The eye will traverse the length of the beds to the area of density, registering the illusion that the garden is broader than it really is.
5. A row of containerised standards, topiary specimens or other plants increasing in

height as they get further away, will also have the effect of shortening the overall view.

6. If you choose bricks for the surface of pathways, remember not to lay them longitudinally!

7. Create illusion with colour. Blue-toned colours tend to recede, so plant vegetables with glaucous foliage – cabbages, purple-leafed and podded dwarf beans – nearest the garden entrance. (If you are trying to do the opposite and make a short garden appear longer, then plant in reverse.) Similarly, a long garden can be foreshortened with the use of bright flowers like nasturtiums, pot marigolds, sunflowers or dahlias, and vice versa.

The careful consideration of aspects such as the foregoing emphasise the desirability of putting pen to paper and *planning* before you rush out to create your potager. Remember, your aim is twofold – to create an edible garden that is not only productive, but also aesthetically pleasing.

Size

Having a small garden does not mean you cannot have an attractive potager; the tiniest of spaces can be divided from a rectangle or square into four smaller beds (see Plan 5). An appealing arrangement of spring onions, dwarf beans, radishes, beetroot and lettuces planted in one of the divisions will yield a surprisingly large harvest. With three other sections left to fill there is still room for slow-to-mature larger plants such as maincrop-potatoes, onions, parsnips, brassicas and leeks.

A highly decorative potager in which repetitive concentric circles create an attractive circular ground plan. An urn containing a small figure is underplanted with herbs and white *Lychnis coronaria alba* to form an attractive centrepiece.

The ground plan of this potager is interesting because it illustrates that formal beds can be created from an irregular shape. Plantings in diagonal rows are bordered by dwarf hedges of box in a roughly triangular bed which is curved on its outer edge. A circular bed with white iris and a container planted with lavender forms a visually pleasing centrepiece.

Suitable shapes

La Quintinie's concern was as much for the pleasing proportions of the garden as for its productivity.

The best figure for a Fruit or Kitchen garden and most convenient for Culture is a beautiful Square of straight angles, being once and a half if not twice as long as 'tis broad . . .

Art of French Vegetable Gardening, Louisa Jones (full details in bibliography)

What he advocates is of course a rectangle in modern gardeners' terminology. The entrance, he advises, should be placed in the short side of the design, facing a broad path extending the whole length of the potager.

Another favourite medieval ground plan, still widely used in the Northern Hemisphere today, is that in which each square within the rectangle is divided into two triangles, with the centre higher than the outside edges. Endless variations of plant texture, height and colour are possible within this basic design, and in the case of the more ornate layouts which follow, it is possible to extract the centre piece from several to form an attractive smaller potager.

For the beginner, the simplest design for a potager layout at ground level is a square or rectangle divided into four equal beds (see Plan 1) and edged with a low hedge of *Buxus sempervirens*, *Lonicera nitida*, or evergreen herbs such as lavender, santolina or rosemary. Within the beds, mange-tout peas, French beans, salsify, salad greens and herbs may be mixed with new varieties of stalwart old favourites – red Brussels sprouts, golden celery, purple-leafed leeks, red or gold-stemmed chards, all presenting a glorious variety of leaf shape, colour, size and texture.

Laying out your design

So to consideration of ground plans for designing and laying out the traditional edible garden. The marking out of the knot or parterre garden is not difficult but it is an exercise which requires care if the results are to look good in years to come. The basic ground layouts for the designs which follow can be set up without the need for complicated geometric calculations. The basic tools required are a supply of wooden pegs and a ball of strong non-stretching string. The design can be scratched into the ground, but a more refined technique makes use of sand

HEDGING PLANTS – BUXUS SEMPERVIRENS
LONICERA NITIDA

PATHWAYS – BRICK, PAVING SLABS,
PEBBLES OR SHINGLE

Plan 1 – Diagonal row concept

This plan illustrates a simple but effective traditional potager design in which one large square is divided into four smaller squares. A further design option is to divide the latter into two triangular beds intersected with narrower pathways, which also avoids the necessity of walking on the soil, which can be a nuisance in wet weather.

The beds may be planted in diagonal rows with edibles of varying heights and colours which makes for interesting patterns and textures, or block-planted with cabbages, cauliflowers, broccoli, etc. The longest rows may be used for one's favourite vegetables and the shorter ones for others. The corners are ideal for single plants like courgettes, for clumps of herbs or vertically grown vegetables such as climbing beans. Main pathways should be a minimum of 1 m (3 ft) wide to allow barrow and easy working access.

The simple geometric layout of Plan 1 allows versatility and flexibility of design; a bowl effect may be achieved by planting the tallest vegetables and herbs on the outside and the lowest in the middle, or by putting them the other way round to create a pyramid effect. Similarly, even though the diagonal rows predominate, the corner of each of the four squares may be cut off to form a separate bed in the middle. Combined, these beds form a circle or diamond shape which will look attractive planted with different salad plants, a colourful patch of edible flowers, or if central height and vertical accent are required, with climbing vegetables on tepees. The suggested planting plan is for the warmer months of the year and would be subject to seasonal fluctuations or personal planting preferences.

trickled out of a bottle. The first set of lines to be marked out is the outer frame. Next comes the centre point, which is located by crossing diagonal lines. Finally come the lines that make up the basic geometrical inner design. Choose a design from the traditional ground-plan layouts which follow and see the marking-out guide on page 22. (More about shapes later.)

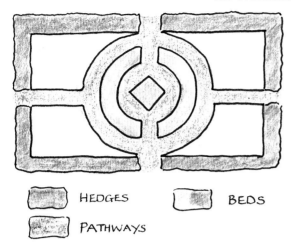

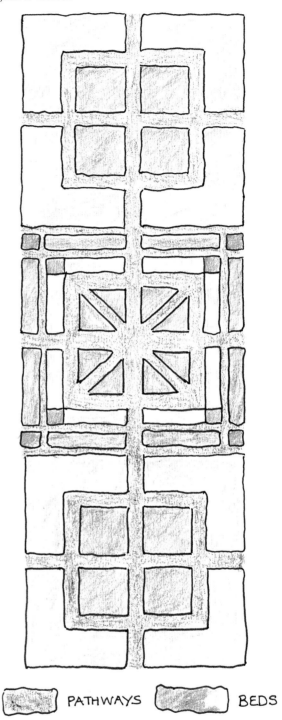

HEDGES   BEDS

PATHWAYS

Plan 2 – A circular design within a rectangle

Created from a rectangle, this plan offers an attractive circular design which becomes divided into a semicircle by the intersection of pathways for easy working and harvesting. The bed at the heart of the design can be another small circle to emphasise the concentric effect of the overall design, or diamond shaped to give an interesting geometric contrast.

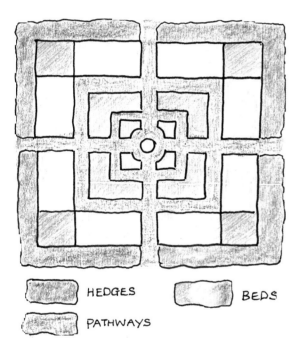

HEDGES   BEDS

PATHWAYS

PATHWAYS   BEDS

Plan 3 – Formed from a square or a rectangle

This is for a more ornate and larger potager and is formed equally well from either a square or a rectangle. The design allows for pathways for easy access to all beds. The central square offers an interesting combination of shapes and could be extracted from the larger design to create an attractive smaller potager.

Plan 4 – A 'three-in-one' layout

This elongated rectangle composed of three squares contains the basic ground-plan layout for one large and ornate potager, or for three separate designs. In each case, the basic geometry is of a square within a square intersected by a pattern of pathways for decorative and utilitarian effect.

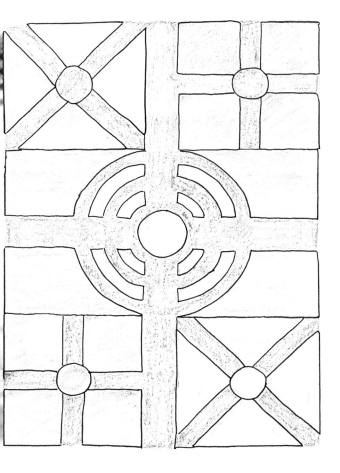

Plan 5 – Traditional ground layouts for the potager

This illustrates a series of geometrical shapes such as squares, triangles and circles. By combining a series of these shapes, plots of any size can be given formality and structure. The centre of the ground plan, the circular design within the rectangle, could be extracted to form an interesting layout, or either of the two square plans standing alone would offer a parterre of traditional design.

Knots and parterres

Knot gardens in ancient days resembled the designs on Persian and Indian carpets in their complexity, and incorporated different types of hedging to produce interweaving colours. The great potager gardens at Versailles and Villandry in France have many such parterres, but this sort of thing is obviously a bit over the top for the modern home potager! It is wiser to settle for a simple design, especially if you are planning to grow herbs, flowers and vegetables together within the one parterre.

Traditional hedging plants for this type of knot garden include grey-foliaged *Santolina chamaecyparissus*, silver germander (*Teucrium fruticans*), dark green box (*Buxus sempervirens*)

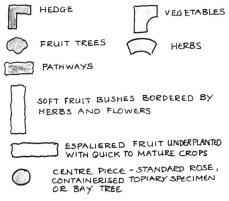

HEDGE

VEGETABLES

FRUIT TREES

HERBS

PATHWAYS

SOFT FRUIT BUSHES BORDERED BY HERBS AND FLOWERS

ESPALIERED FRUIT UNDERPLANTED WITH QUICK TO MATURE CROPS

CENTRE PIECE – STANDARD ROSE, CONTAINERISED TOPIARY SPECIMEN OR BAY TREE

Plan 6 – For a formal garden

Plan 6 features a ground plan with an interesting combination of geometric shapes within a large square. The four elongated rectangles at the outer edges of the potager offer scope for soft-fruit bushes or espaliered fruits and vines, or beds for herbs. Provision is made for space for a fruit tree at each of the four corners. As with plan three, the centre square extracted would make an attractive traditional potager design in its own right.

AN OPTION FOR A MORE FORMAL
LOOK WOULD BE TO EDGE THE BEDS
TO CORRESPOND WITH THE OUTER HEDGE

Plan 7 – A simple parterre

Medieval gardens were always very formal in design, growing vegetables, herbs and flowers together in rectangular and circular beds. These designs adapt well to modern gardens where limited space makes informal designs difficult. Knot gardens and parterres were popular in England and Europe as far back as the fifteenth century. Plan 7 is based on a medieval design for a simple parterre, and like all the basic ground-plan layouts in this section can be adapted in size to fit the largest or smallest of gardens.

and gold *Lonicera nitida* 'Baggeson's Gold'. The combination of colour contrast and careful clipping produces the illusion that the hedges weave over and under each other where they meet, rather than simply butting up against each other. Young hedging plants should be grown about 15 cm (6 in) apart. Pinching out the developing shoots will encourage the bushy growth required to form a dwarf hedge.

Marking out the potager ground plan

Once you have chosen your basic design, draw the plan to scale on a sheet of graph paper. Prepare the area by digging, removing perennial weeds and incorporating manure or compost. Finally, rake the soil level. Transfer your design to the land, using a series of pegs and twine for the straight lines, and sand trickled from a bottle for the circles or curved lines. It is best to use sand because lines painstakingly measured out and scratched into the earth can be washed away by a shower of rain!

With a square or rectanglar shape it is easy to check that the sides are exactly at right angles by measuring from corner to corner and adjusting if necessary. Find the centre point by measuring and marking with lengths of twine two lines at

right angles from corner to corner and place a cane at the exact centre point (where the lines cross). The cane should remain in position throughout, since it determines the position of all future measurements.

Tie a length of string to the cane, measuring the exact circumference or dimensions for the centrepiece of the design. Extend the twine outwards around the cane and mark the outline of the desired shape for the centrepiece. If solid edgings are to be used along the pathways to prevent pebbles, shingles or other softer pathway mediums from working their way into the beds, they should be built in at this stage (see Chapter 3).

When pathways have been constructed, the hedging plants should be set 15–25 cm (6–10 in) apart along the outlines of the design marked by sand and strings. When the linear confines of the design have been completed, dig over the areas designated as beds and finally plant chosen vegetables, flowers and herbs.

Bed-shaped templates

If you wish to build up a design with a repeated pattern of beds of the same shape and size, it is worth taking the time to make a template. Draw

Repeated topiary specimens, clipped hedges and inter-secting brick pathways laid in a simple but bold pattern combine to give this larger potager strong design, further emphasised by the patterns created by orderly rows of young beans and block-planted lettuces.

the shape onto a large piece of cardboard, scrap wood or plastic, with the digging area outlined in the middle. The template will be particularly useful if the beds are to be cut out of a grassed area. All you need to do is lay and peg down the template in position and cut round the inside edges with a spade before removing the turf. It is also helpful to make the frame's edges the same width as your intended paths, for easy location of adjacent beds. Use a set square to ensure your angles are correct.

Designing the potager – formal or informal?

On the whole it is wiser to aim for a certain amount of formality in the basic design of your potager. In a design which is too informal many of the larger plants need support if they are not to flop on top of other low-growing crops, and it is easier to provide this when the edibles are grown in rows or clumps. Another problem is that harvesting produce can leave gaps that detract from the appearance of the potager, so the overall design must be strong enough to carry off bare patches of soil which will exist until the next crop is sown. This is why prac-tised potagists choose a symmetrically balanced design.

Achieving symmetry

Formal gardens are in vogue again because gardeners have realised that formality does not mean rigidity, that informal plantings are enhanced by strict linear confines, and that symmetry itself is pleasing to the eye. Within the potager, this does not mean that each bed must be a mirror image of the others, which would be both boring and produce a huge glut of identical produce! A pleasing balance in the planting scheme is achieved by choosing similar colours and heights in different plants rather than in using identical plants. For example, the feathery tops of carrots and the foliage of Japanese mustard look alike at a distance, as do parsnips and celery and many other edibles.

Another fun way to achieve symmetry is by the careful placing of plants or structures to achieve vertical accents. Climbing plants on tepees, standard rose bushes or rosemary, clipped bay trees, or containerised topiary specimens placed at identical intervals in each section of the potager will create a sense of unity and help you give an impression of symmetry even if all the plants in the beds beneath are different.

The simplest design for achieving symmetry is a basic square or rectangle, divided into four parts by a wide central path and slightly narrower side paths. The wider path provides a strong axis in the traditional European style, and further emphasis may be obtained by using espaliered fruit trees, or a sequence of clipped box shapes to border these paths. The bigger the potager, the bigger the plants can be, which allows the division of each major part into its own smaller pattern.

Scale

As with planning any garden, the most important aspect of planning the potager is that of proportion and scale. As a basic principle, all the components of the design – the beds, the paths, the boundary hedges or walls – should be on the same scale. A small potager with high boundary enclosures will look cramped no matter how hard one works at planting plans. The same area

An intricate network of brick pathways of varying widths creates an interesting ground layout in this larger potager and forms a striking design feature. The pathways outline beds of varying sizes and shapes planted with a wide variety of herbs and vegetables, offering a pleasing diversity of foliage colour, form and texture.

Brick pathways outline a ground plan design composed of two square beds enclosed by two L-shaped beds. The inner beds are intersected with narrower brick pathways for ease of access and harvesting. An ornamental archway planted with the climbing rose 'Phyllis Bide' spans the main pathway through the potager, and espalier fences divide the front garden from the rear.

with low enclosures, narrow paths and small beds containing plants of a more compact growth habit will look neat and spacious. Similarly, a large garden looks best with high enclosures, wide paths and big beds. Filling it with an elaborate pattern of small beds and complex paths will produce a fussy, claustro-phobic effect.

If you prefer small beds for ease of access and maintenance, it is wise to group them into block patterns which can be repeated in rhythmic com-position round the rest of the garden. An alter-native method of incorporating small beds into a large-scale plan is to subdivide some of the larger beds with small pathways. This will facilitate the growing of large crops such as brassicas, and the smaller beds can be occupied with more compact edibles. But care must be taken that these subdi-vided beds do not unbalance the unity of the overall design. The ground plan layouts in this chapter illustrate that the most suitable position for them is in the centre of the potager where they will balance each other, or in the centre of each big block of beds where they can echo the pattern of the main block.

Squares are easy

When it comes to the actual shape of beds, as the ground plans show, squares are definitely the easiest to work with. If the potager itself is square, it can be divided into smaller squares, triangles, rectangles, L-shapes, or any combina-tion of these shapes. Each of the four squares within the main square allows plenty of planting scope. Even a square with 1 m (3 ft) sides could be a mini-potager of its own, with a 30 cm (1 ft) square of medium-tall plants such as broad beans, Florence fennel or a single tomato in the middle, and two 15 cm (6 in) wide rows of lower plants such as lettuces, carrots or beetroot. Or it could have climbing edibles on tepees in each corner. A bed of this size will easily provide enough nutrients for half a dozen runner beans, four tomatoes or cucumbers, with a quick crop of radishes or lettuces harvested before they are overshadowed by the beans.

Triangles and diamonds

A small equilateral triangle serves the purpose of housing three tepee poles for climbing edibles. In general, small triangles are best used for

The simple clean lines of the ground layout of this potager are emphasised and complemented by elegant ornamental structures. The beds have been formed from elongated diamond and lozenge shapes, their apices skilfully emphasised and filled with wedges of clipped box. Block plantings such as the red lettuce (at left) fulfil the same purpose when the points or angles of irregular shaped beds require filling.

block plantings. The more acute the angles are, the more difficult it is to plant the angles so they maintain their shape. The acute angle needs to be full of plants which do not flop about, so you must either provide support, which is labour intensive, or use very small plants such as salad stuffs. The same problems apply to elongated diamonds or lozenge shapes; they have acutely awkward angles to fill unless the aim is for a tapestry effect of plants in solid blocks.

L-shapes

L-shapes are much more useful and easy to handle. They can be thick or thin, equal or unequal sided, and they fit neatly round a square or a rectangle as shown in ground plans 3 and 4. Two of them will interlock with each other to make a T-shape or four back to back will make a cross. They are after all, no more than two rectangles joined together and can be planted with interesting variations on any of the rectangular themes. The only difficulty with L-shapes is how to get long rows around corners if you

don't wish to 'mitre' the corner. The best alternative is to make the corner into a separate square as in plans 3 and 4. The planting of a taller growing plant such as a tomato, or a tepee of climbing beans, will give vertical accent and create a focal point, and the original row of vegetables can be continued on the other side.

The fact that the inside edge of an L-shaped bed is shorter than the outside – the thicker the bed the greater the difference – can be useful if you want to grow a smaller quantity of a particular vegetable, such as garlic in an onion bed.

Rectangles

Rectangles, like squares, are easy shapes to deal with, from both the pattern planning and planting aspects. Two rectangles of identical size could be used without any other shapes to make a complete potager. This idea has merit because one is dealing with a known quantity all the time when digging, manuring or planting. The rectangles can be planted with masses, blocks or rows, and the rows can be long, short or diagonal. Two rectangles alongside each other with opposite diagonal rows would make a herringbone pattern, or a series of rectangles could be used to make other herringbone patterns. Intersected with paths of bricks laid in a pleasing pattern, this simple design is one which has maintained its popularity from medieval times.

Block planting for curved beds

All the beds discussed so far have straight sides. There is no reason why beds with curving sides should not be employed but they are best filled with block planting because it is difficult to deal with curved rows in any other way. Curved patterns may be created, and if the plants are planted to touch but not overwhelm each other, the outer leaves will form cover to keep the sun off the surface of the beds and to suppress weeds. Block planting also offers the option of creating a chequer board effect by using alternate plants of different colours, perhaps red and gold beetroot, or green and purple dwarf beans or, best of all, lettuces in mixes of red and green.

Planting plans

Having read this chapter and selected your basic ground-plan design, you need to consider the practicalities of growing the actual plants. If you try to put plants together which have different cultivation requirements, or which will be vastly disproportionate in size, there are bound to be disasters, leaving glaring 'gap-toothed' effects in the overall plan! Even with a simple design it is worth taking a few minutes with pencil and pad to make a planting plan. Use a set of coloured pencils, or devise a set of symbols to indicate size, colour and texture of the plants required, and start by marking in all the obvious viewing places. Add some dotted lines to indicate which areas can be seen from each of these places, but remember that the areas will alter as various plants reach maturity.

This potager, established within an open lawn, has to look good from all angles. The garden is also viewed from the terrace and house above, so taking time in the initial stages to plan for block plantings and foliage combinations which will present a pleasing tapestry effect is well worth the effort.

Left: A great deal of planning at ground level has gone into this beautifully laid out and well proportioned potager. Lavender-edged brick pathways create symmetrically appealing patterns and outline beds of varying geometric shapes.

Opposite: This stunning potager is full of fun and dynamic design concepts. Vegetative support poles and seats of vibrant blue create a dramatic juxtaposition with bold flower colours and with the archway and framework of traditional woven willow.

Allow optional plant choices. Flexibility and a supply of back-up plants will allow you to defeat the worst vagaries of the weather, pests and diseases, and of course gaps left by harvesting. This last is especially important because the greater proportion of edibles are annuals, and in one short growing season there will be no time to rectify mistakes. Edible plants, unlike our long-suffering shrubs and perennials, do not take being upwardly mobile in their stride.

It is also a good idea to make a very rough plan for the next season's crop so you will be able to remember at a glance which vegetables you should be sowing to replace those you are harvesting. This will avoid large patches of bare earth and the resulting unwelcome drop in productivity. These rough plans are invaluable also for practising plant and crop rotation, since the soil will soon become exhausted if you continue to plant the same crop consecutively in one area. (See Chapter 6.)

If you have an informal potager consisting of one or a few large beds, or if your formal layout consists of a few basic shapes, planning the planting will be straightforward. If your ambitions have led you to an elaborate layout with multiple beds it is wise to block them out on graph paper, which will help you assess how many of each plant you need to fill each area. Remember to mark which area of the potager faces north (or south if you are in the Northern Hemisphere) – this is very important for deciding where to locate taller edibles and those which prefer either sun or shade.

The fun starts now with a browse through the seedsmen's catalogues to decide what exciting edibles to try. Plan for maximum visual impact by deciding which vegetables will complement each other colourwise, and do try to observe the height each is expected to attain at maturity. It is boring to say the least playing hunt the (weak and spindly) radishes beneath the huge leaves of the broccoli. Pick up your wooden pegs, string, bottles of sand, then go forth, measure up and move on to framework construction in Chapter 2.

CONSTRUCTING THE FRAMEWORK

Pathways

Suitable mediums for pathways include bricks, pavers, concrete slabs, gravel, pea shingle, pebbles, bark, grass. Paths should be a minimum of 65 cm (2 ft 6 in) wide for comfortable walking, but 1 m (3 ft) is ideal for wheelbarrow access. If pathways are to be of grass, remember to allow for the width of the mower you will be using.

Pathways in the potager should be firm, and provide easy access to the beds for maintenance and harvesting. Gravel, scoria, bark or crushed oyster shell are less expensive than bricks or custom-made pavers, but do allow weed growth

Opposite: This healthy and productive potager presents a framework of strong design features which are both aesthetically pleasing and utilitarian.
Above: Stone pavers set in gravel and edged with weathered sleepers create both bold design features and a strong framework in the centre of this small potager.

and eventually break down and need replacing. Grass pathways are rarely satisfactory. They require regular mowing, are labour intensive, and become worn and muddy in wet weather.

Old bricks are the traditional paving medium for potager pathways and walls and in addition to being long lasting, they are by far the most attractive – but they can be costly. Demand often exceeds supply and those who have them can name their price. Many are 'uncleaned' bricks, that is, with mortar and cement still adhering, which the purchaser must remove. Be warned! This entails long hours with a chisel, hammer and scrapers removing the old mortar, but the aged, mellow ambience the bricks create when laid is (probably) worth it.

If you are not a purist and are content to use modern custom-made bricks, the price (ironically) is a little less than for demolition bricks, and they soon mellow to the softer tones of the latter. If a less than flourishing bank account rules out the use of old bricks, and less noble materials like concrete blocks or paving must be used, their harsher facades can be softened with creeping thymes and sedums.

Edgings

All pathways made of softer walking mediums must have a solid edging, or the bark, pebbles, shingle, or oyster shell will find their way into the potager beds with all speed. Railway sleepers are strong, long lasting and aesthetically pleasing. The local demolition yard will offer a variety of timbers such as floor boards which make sturdy edgings of good height, but it is essential that they are in good condition and pleasing to look at. Custom-made lengths of jointed and ribbed wooden garden edging of varying heights are also efficient for dividing the pathways or beds, and weather to an attractive patina. Brick, stone or slab pathways look best edged with bricks or tiles in a slanted vertical position. A row of upright bricks laid in a 'soldier' row is also an effective alternative.

Dimensions

When you are planning the dimensions of your paths, remember that bricks and most paving slabs come in standard sizes. Decide what medium you want to use, and in what pattern, then check on these sizes and the recommended spacing before doing your maths to arrive at the final width. If you intend to do this work yourself, invest in a proper pair of padded strap-on knee pads. I laid pathways in my potager involving some 2000 bricks and even with deluxe pads had, in the end, to restrict myself to laying 50–60 bricks (about 1 m, 3 ft) per day!

Laying edgings

Whether your finished design incorporates the use of solid edgings or not, all pathways need to be constructed within an initial framework in the first stages. Using a series of wooden pegs and twine, measure out the dimensions of the

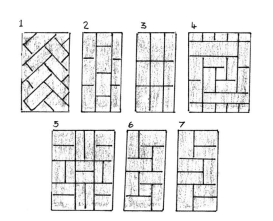

Brick patterns

Bricks can be laid flat or on edge, in straight rows or various patterns. Since a standard brick is half as wide as it is long, there are a number of easy patterns involving blocks of two or three bricks. These are known as basketweave, and allow an easy calculation of widths. One of the most elegant patterns is herringbone, but it is more difficult to lay since it involves skilful cutting to fill in the small triangles at the edges.

Laying a brick pathway

Once the outer framework of your brick path is firmly in place, put down approximately 7 cm (2¼ in) of 'hardcore' (brick rubble or broken concrete) which must be compacted by rolling and stamping, then a layer of sand or 'lean mix' – about 3–4 parts of sand to 1 of cement. Lay the bricks or slabs on top in desired pattern, using a spirit level to check that they are level, then fill the gaps with dry lean mix, brushing it firmly into all the cracks.

paths and dig them out, level and flatten. Hammer in the wooden pegs at regular intervals along the pathway and lay durable strips of timber *inside* them and nail them together. Set the desired pathway within the framework.

Above: Skilfully positioned bricks have been used in this semi-formal potager to indicate change of direction, as contrasting edging, and have shaped an attractive diamond-shaped centrepiece.

Left: Old bricks of irregular shapes create the pathway in this appealing potager. In order to maintain the path at consistent width the bricks have been spaced with mortar and bordered on the outer edge with others of regular size laid end to end.

Laying paving slabs

Paving slabs should be embedded in mortar, a mixture of cement and lime or both, with sand and water used to hold the bricks or stones together.

After excavating the pathway, level the soil and lay down a layer of hardcore (brick rubble or broken concrete). Use a tamper or roller to crush it flat. Then use a section of plank to

Left: This attractive potager illustrates the effectiveness of pathways formed from plain paving slabs. Laid end to end they direct the feet into the garden, and side by side form a circular centrepiece of strong design at the heart of the potager. Their pale colours are complemented by plantings of blue pansies and cineraria 'Silver Dust' beneath the sundial. The circlet of pebbles ringing the plants is a pleasing and unusual design feature.

Below: Terracotta-coloured slabs edged with curved bricks set in upright 'soldier' fashion make a simple but attractive pathway through a potager herb garden.

spread a layer of ash, lean mix concrete (1 part cement to 3–4 parts sand) or similar fine material over the hard core as this will bind it together. Trowel the mortar over the area of the first slab. Make sure that it is spread to correct height, with the necessary slope for drainage, by checking it against a string guideline. To ensure even spacing between slabs temporarily insert pieces of wood of uniform size. Tap the slabs into the desired position, using a spirit level to check the correct levels.

Laying pathways of shingle, bark, scoria, pebbles, gravel, etc.

If you have chosen one of these softer walking mediums, follow the construction processes as for solid edgings, and when your pathway is dug out and levelled, ensure that all troublesome perennial weeds are removed. Lay sheets of heavy-duty polythene to prevent weed regrowth and fill with the desired walking medium.

Above left: Pine needles provide a softer walking medium and an appealing textured surface for the pathways in this potager.
Above right: Fine grey gravel and river-washed rocks combine to create a cool and attractive pathway and bed edgings. Their pale colour provides an effective foil to the rich dark green of the mature trees.

Aromatic pathways

Herbs such as creeping thymes or camomiles, which release their pungent perfumes when trodden on, are so delightful that one can tolerate having to hand weed them now and again. Unlike grass pathways, they have the added virtue of not requiring mowing, but they may need solid edgings to prevent them 'creeping' into the beds.

Above: This medieval woodcut shows a gardener working with a raised bed, in which the earth is banked up behind retaining boards. Raised beds are ideal for growing herbs and vegetables because they ensure good drainage.

Building raised beds

Problems common to many vegetable gardens include impoverished soil and poor drainage. Both these problems are easily overcome if the gardener employs raised beds, a horticultural practice made widely popular by Austrian horticulturist Rudolph Steiner, who instituted it in Switzerland in the early 1900s. The beds are filled with soil enriched with organic fertilisers such as manure and compost. The height of the beds and the loose structure of the well fed, well

Right: A steep or sloping site usually requires terracing and in this case the construction of a sturdy pergola and stoutly built raised beds provide the garden with both a strong framework and attractive design features.

conditioned soil promotes free drainage and good plant growth.

Edging mediums for raised beds include old railway sleepers, round poles, breeze blocks, or any lengths of tanalised durable timber. The size, height and shape of the beds depends upon individual requirements. Construction is not difficult, requiring accurate measurement and cutting of corresponding lengths of wood, some long strong nails for corner joints and a few wooden reinforcing pegs if long planks are being used. In the case of round poles being stacked vertically as an edging, nailing may be difficult and it is sometimes more convenient to wire them together.

Vertical accents and ornamental structures

Vegetable gardening entails constructing one or more broad flat surfaces, then laying these out with a plant mosaic, but every garden exists in three dimensions and to achieve maximum ornamental effect, there must be contrasts of height above the patterning at ground level. The garden's

Above left: Raised beds arranged in an unusual ground plan pattern create bold design features in this beautifully planned small potager.
Above centre: The basic framework under construction around this potager incorporates raised beds, terraced levels and a sturdy pergola. The design of this small vegetable garden is particularly suited to a steep or sloping site.
Above right: Wide pathways of grey gravel allow easy access for working and harvesting raised beds in this low maintenance edible garden.

walls and hedges will already be providing vertical presence, but these need to be emphasised by other upright structures. These may take the form of temporary plant material (tall edibles such as globe artichokes, sweetcorn, climbing beans, tall growing herbs, etc.) or semi-permanent constructions such as attractive plant supports or espalier frames. They may fulfil the dual role of being both ornamental and providing vertical accent as in the case of structures such as statuary, sun dials, fountains, bird baths and topiary in containers. The latter, placed at the centre of converging pathways, at their beginning and ending, entrance or exit, create an excellent accent point for marking an axis or vista.

In areas where winters are more severe, vertical accents may be provided in season by citrus or dwarf fruit trees in large containers which may be moved to positions of shelter when necessary.

Last but not least for providing decorative vertical interest in the potager is the fun figure of a scarecrow — mock human figures which have been employed since medieval times to keep birds away from crops. The family can give full reign to their imagination in dressing simple wooden frames. Last season I was treated to a most dramatic *Phantom of the Opera* figure complete with dashing red cloak (an old bed-spread), but the one which tickled visitors most was a punk figure with spiked and aerosol-sprayed multicoloured straw hair, 'shades' and a pig ring through his 'nose'!

An archway of lashed bamboo canes and a frame to the rear left fulfil the dual roles of providing vertical accents and attractive support structures for sweet peas, nasturtiums and other climbing crops.

A basic scarecrow 'skeleton'

The sketch gives a guide to the construction of a scarecrow 'skeleton'. The framework may be made of any pieces of old timber, but the centre stake should be strong enough to be hammered into the ground and tanalised for durability.

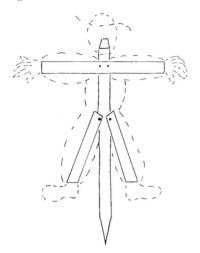

The scarecrow's head may be made from flesh-coloured fabric and stuffed with hay or straw. Hammer the skeleton (see diagram) firmly into the ground, place the head upon the top of the stake, dress the scarecrow and stuff the garments with hay or straw. Tie the ends of the sleeves and pants to stop the stuffing falling out. Like all vertical accents, the scarecrow must be placed with care so that the shade cast on surrounding plantings will not be too dense.

In many cases, shade will be just what the potager gardener may be seeking. In this case, vines bearing edible fruit, or climbing roses on archways or pergolas, make most desirable vertical structures in or around the garden. Solid constructions and plantings such as these vastly improve the aesthetics of the decorative edible garden, regardless of size. The utilitarian vegetable plot has the unfortunate reputation of being strictly monotonous and horizontal, with all plantings laid out in rigid rows. The modern potager gardener has a wide choice of ornamental structures and plant material at his or her disposal so that a happy balance between simplicity and variety can be obtained.

Above: A well dressed scarecrow watches over a luxuriantly productive bed of beet, leeks and broccoli bordered by drifts of white lobelias.
Below: These amusing 'potpersons' are definitely the focal point of this edible garden. This informal potager is enclosed by a simple wooden fence which gives it a sunny open aspect and layers of wood chippings have been used to cover pathways.

Structural supports for veges

Medium-height plants such as tomatoes can be tied to wires, netting or mesh stretched between two posts. Larger varieties of tomatoes can also be grown inside a cylinder of wire or plastic mesh attached to a single post. Taller varieties of peas will cling to any form of mesh, but their delicate tendrils will not be able to get a good hold on anything as thick as a bamboo pole. Traditional pea and bean-sticks are comprised of vertical rows of prunings of twiggy branches.

Another useful plant support is some frames of wire-netting to stretch between battens, each with a leg at the back to support the frame at an angle. These are particularly useful for cucum-

A number of ornamental structural supports are featured in this large formal vegetable garden, including twin tepees of stout wooden sticks to maximise planting space in the front bed.

bers or gherkins which will otherwise ramble over a wide area. Lower plants with a tendency to dangle their fruits or pods on the ground can most easily be supported by a bamboo pole running horizontally each side of the row, raised to the appropriate height with bricks or blocks of wood. Although a tunnel of wire-netting is often suggested as a useful support for low plants, this tends to make it difficult to weed and pick items that grow inside the netting and provides shelter for mice and slugs.

Vertical bamboo canes lashed together across a horizontal central runner create a support frame for climbing beans. To the right old-fashioned purple sweet peas grow over a series of ornamental metal hoops.

Wherever poles or stakes are used, they should include some method of 'blunting' the top to avoid eye injury. Old tennis balls, plastic bottles or small flower pots are all usable, or with aesthetics in mind and cash in hand you can splash out on ceramic figures designed specifically for this purpose!

Constructing frames

To construct a basic support frame for climbing vegetables, or a frame on which to train espaliered fruit trees or vines, you will need the following materials and tools.

4 or more (depending on length of frame required) stout 60 x 80 mm (2 in x 3 in) posts
Strong wire
Strong hooks with enclosed eyes
Bamboo canes or lightweight twiggy tree branches
Drill with a fine bit
Pliers
Post-hole borer or spade
Mallet

Method

Drill holes in end posts for insertion of eye hooks. Drill holes through centre posts for threading through of wire – these must obviously correspond with the placing of eye hooks in edge posts. Between 6–8 vertical rows placed approximately 18 cm (7 in) apart will give a waist-high frame which will make easy working for vegetables. If the frame is to be used to espalier fruit, support a vine or form a concealing vegetative boundary, the hooks can be placed much further apart, but the supporting wooden posts will need to be taller.

Sink posts firmly into the ground at regularly spaced intervals. Thread wire through hooks, then through holes in centre posts and strain wire to ensure firm tension. Sink bamboo canes or twiggy branches either side of wires. These are to give the climbing vegetables added support, and to help train the shape of young fruit trees. In either case they will need replacing when the crop matures, or may be removed as the branches of the young trees mature enough to fan out along the wires.

If a really tall strong frame is required, this may be achieved with the use of custom-made steel posts which already have holes drilled for instant insertion of wire. These are not so aesthetically pleasing in an ornamental vegetable garden but, unlike wooden posts, have an extended life because they do not rot.

See Chapter 3 for methods of training fruit trees as cordons or espaliers.

Tepees, towers and archways

Twiggy branches stuck firmly into the ground, their tops arched inwards to form a vault, also form inexpensive, efficient and attractive supports for peas and beans. A similar classic support is a tepee of tall bamboo stakes tied together at the top.

Another popular structure is the tepee tower built of four wooden stakes screwed together at the top and reinforced by wooden cross pieces at the base. A permanent or long-lived structure, it has the additional virtue of being movable whenever seasonal or planting plans dictate, but can also be used to support permanent plantings such as climbers, vines or roses. Do remember to use tanalised wood for greater durability.

To ensure that the wooden tepee does not topple under the weight of the crop or in high wind, the base is pegged down with heavy-duty, long-length tent pegs, two crossed at each corner. The basic 4-stake teepee design, which is adequate for crops such as climbing beans, may be enhanced with trellis panels to give added support to cucurbits or other more ornamental climbers. The tepee may also be placed on top of a wooden planter box for container plantings where space is at a premium.

If you have a home handyperson in the family, bribe him or her to put together a series of these tripods of varying heights and widths for you. If no handyperson is forthcoming, worry not. I have managed to build several of these for myself. The basic design can even be scaled down to accommodate perennials, and if you can find the time or patience to paint the tripods to match various areas of the garden, they look very upmarket and expensive when in fact they cost very little to produce. Screw a wooden ball or finial on top for the ultimate elegance!

The beauty of growing 'vertical veg' is that the ground beneath the tripods can be planted with other edibles such as squash, salad stuffs, etc., which will not interfere with the pea or bean crop above.

A pleasingly natural looking archway may be constructed by positioning two stands of slender pliable branches (willow is a traditional favourite) opposite each other and then bending and tieing their tops together overhead.

The prolific small rose 'Phyllis Bide' scrambles up the metal archways marking the entrance and exit of this edible garden. Vegetable beds on the right are bordered by espaliered fruit trees on a post-and-wire frame such as that described on page 40. Espalier frames not only maximise cropping in minimum space but create useful dividing elements between different garden areas.

CHAPTER 3

ENCLOSING THE GARDEN

Establishing shelter

Successful vegetable gardening requires a site offering maximum sunshine and protection from prevailing winds – in other words, a clever combination of exposure and enclosure. This implies a wall, fence or hedging along at least one side of the chosen plot, if not along all four sides.

Traditional enclosures for the potager include brick walls, hedges, picket or wooden fences, cordons of fruit or vines trained on wires or frames, and stands of soft fruit bushes. In addition to providing shelter, solid enclosures offer the additional bonus of providing support for climbing edibles. This increases the productive surface of the garden since vertical planting is practised. Less permanent plantings like melons, squashes and cucumbers are easy to train on netting, frames, trellises, or against a solid vertical support.

Most gardeners would give their eye teeth to have a vegetable garden enclosed by mellow brick walls like those of ancient potagers. If you will settle for nothing less, be aware that even a wall of modest proportions takes an astonishing amount of costly bricks – and while laying a brick pathway is well within the capabilities of the home gardener, laying a wall takes professional skill and expertise.

If you do not want hedges as an enclosure because of the trimming involved, custom-made wooden fence palings or frames are the best option.

Opposite: The mellow Cotswold stone walls enclosing this grand formal potager also provide support for espaliered fruit.
Above: Fashioned from lengths of wood, rustic wooden gates provide a strong design feature, in juxtaposition to the discreet wire fences enclosing the garden.

Left: Frames of willow prunings woven in a traditional manner enclose this edible garden. An archway of lashed wood will support climbing crops later in the season.
Below: Closely woven twiggy prunings lashed to an outer framework of stout branches create an archway for this edible garden. Tall bottlebrush trees (*Callistemon* spp.) provide a colourful and unusual hedge and smaller plants in the garden are sheltered by beds of luxuriant looking broad beans.

Gates

Walled gardens are often further enhanced by entrances featuring ornamental gateways. Wrought-iron and aluminium lacework gates are attractive, if costly, but once purchased they will outlast the garden and probably its owner. On the other hand, a little imagination, an auction, or a foray through demolition yards can yield gates of both wood and metal that cost less and make innovative additions to the potager.

The head and foot of an old iron bedstead placed at the entrance and exit of an elongated brick pathway can draw the eye along a vista that is both pleasing and dramatic. During a recent holiday in France I visited a potager approached through a wooden gate with palings arranged in graduating height to create a semi-circle at its upper edge. The circle was completed by the addition of a semicircular arch of wood joined to the gate posts, thus framing the garden and drawing the eye to the terracotta tiled roof of a garden shed beyond. The basic design was

simple enough for any (fairly!) handy home gardener to engineer and, painted a subtle grey-green, made a most elegant and impressive entrance to the edible garden.

Archways

Well established potagers often have archways cut through mature hedges of yew, macrocarpa, hornbeam or beech. But if you are creating a new ornamental vegetable garden (and do not have half a century or so to spare) you will have to settle for an archway of decorative trellis, metal or timber – all available at a relatively inexpensive sum from local suppliers. Trellis frames come in standard sizes and are available with patterning of squares, diamonds and diagonals. If you prefer a more natural look, the potager may also be enclosed with archways of bent willow branches or tall twiggy prunings woven into a vaulted arch, as discussed in the last chapter.

Right: Enclosed to the left by a tall hedge of dark green privet, the pathway of this formal potager is spanned by a hooped ornamental metal archway draped with sweet peas. Lower hedges of box enclose beds to the right and pathways of cream shingle complement the darker foliage of the privet and box.

Temporary enclosures or dividers

Taller vegetables such as sweetcorn, cardoons, globe and Jerusalem artichokes, amaranths, broad beans and sunflowers, also taller herbs such as angelica, bronze fennel and borage, may all be used as temporary screens or enclosures. Stands of climbing beans and peas can easily form a curtain between various areas of the potager. Grown on twiggy branches or custom-made tripods they also form an attractive centrepiece. Topiary specimens, standardised lavender, rosemary, bay trees, dwarf fruit trees, citrus, etc., in containers, may also be used as instant screens or dividers.

Aromatic and flowering edgings for beds and paths

One of the most creative possibilities in potager design is the use of plants as edgers along paths or around beds. These can be temporary and seasonal, e.g., parsley, beetroot, red and green

basils, red-leafed lettuces or marigolds, etc., or more permanent and comprised of evergreen herbs such as lavender, blue-flowered rosemary, hyssop, or of silvery cotton lavender or helichrysums. Hardy shrubby herbs such as these give sterling service, but can be short lived. They become woody and sparse or begin to die back. It is irritating to say the least when one plant dies out, giving the hedge a gap-toothed appearance, but the problem is easily dealt with. All grow easily from cuttings, and taking a few minutes extra at the time of trimming to push a few into the ground beneath the parent hedge soon produces sturdy new growth.

A particularly pleasing colour scheme of plum-purple, pewter and silver is created by combining a foliage edging of purple-leafed sage, *Salvia officinalis*, with a lilac-flowered lavender interspersed with clumps of chives with rosy-mauve ball heads.

Rosemary (*Rosmarinus officinalis*) makes a hardy edging and clips into a neat, compact hedge. It has the added bonus of bearing its delightful silvery-blue flowers in winter when little else is in bloom.

Silver germander (*Teucrium fruticans*) also clips into an attractive hedge but requires good drainage. It is satisfyingly quick to grow and thus needs fairly regular clipping.

Lavender (*Lavandula angustifolia*), the most commonly found lavender variety, also comes as *L. a.* 'Alba' and *L. a.* 'Rosea', but these are less hardy than their robust blue-flowered relative. *L. stoechas pedunculata*, with fat purple-blue spikes, is adaptable to most soils and even copes with clay where drainage is poor. For low edges or hedges *L. angustifolia* comes in dwarf culti- vars such as *L. a.* 'Hidcote', *L. a.* 'Loddon Pink', *L. a.* 'Nana Alba', and *L. a.* 'Munstead'. **French lavender** (*L. dentata*) is an excellent edger when a taller hedge is required. Robust in growth, it is an attractive, hardy plant with grey-green foliage and soft lavender-blue flower spikes borne over long periods. In warmer areas, if kept lightly trimmed, it will flower for most of

the year. These traditional lavender stalwarts are universally available.

Santolina (*Santolina chamaecyparissus*) is also called cotton lavender, but it is not a true lavender. This dainty shrub has finely dissected silver foliage and clusters of golden ball-like flowers. Cold hardy, it grows to approximately 70 cm (2 ft 3 in).

All four of these hardy herbs are daughters of sun-baked Mediterranean slopes and abhor wet feet. They will tolerate poor soils but require a position of full sun and good drainage,

Left: Vegetable beds are edged with luxuriant borders of lavender on their inner edges and with neat balls of box on the outer. In addition to providing symmetry, standard gooseberry bushes either side of the path create an attractive and unusual design feature.
Below: In this informal potager vegetable beds are enclosed with a strong outer edging of scoured stones and a softer plant edging of forget-me-nots within. The potager is well protected by hedges of mature shrubs and trees.

so it is wise to plant thirsty edibles such as tomatoes and leafy salad stuffs in the inner potager, rather than immediately beneath these herb hedgings.

Plant edgers are complemented in their various ways by the types of plants chosen to grow behind them. Feathery, clear green carrot foliage, for example, mixed with red oak-leaf lettuce or variegated thyme creates a pleasing tiered effect of a mixture of varying leaf textures and colour tones.

Certain types of vegetables and fruits can themselves be used as temporary but fun edgings and outliners. Favourites of mine are the many varieties of red, gold and green capsicums and chillies which are compact in growth and offer vibrant colour. A border of strawberries will delight as an easily harvested edging alongside a pathway. Plant edgings also provide the opportunity to experiment with companion planting and many medicinal and aromatic varieties can be employed for this purpose. Chives, for example, with lavender pom-pom heads, feverfew with daisy-like flowers, or massed herbs provide both attractive and insect-repelling edgings.

Hedges

If a new potager garden is to be planned on an exposed site, an innovative living wall may be created by planting a shelter belt of mixed evergreen and deciduous shrubs and trees, producing not only a wind screen but flowers and fruit as well. Vegetative windbreaks filter, absorb and deflect wind energy, and experience has shown that the most effective plantings are those that modify the wind's force, rather than those forming an impenetrable barrier. When the wind is totally deflected, with perhaps a solid fence or wall, it can cause severe erosion and turbulence in adjacent areas. There is always the danger that as the plants top the fence they will receive the full force of the wind and suffer root rock or have their heads torn off.

A mix of hardy plants such as abelia, colutea, buddleia (will bring the butterflies), coprosmas, conifers, pittosporums, photinia, dogwoods (coloured stems in winter), cotoneasters (polished red or yellow berries), corokias, akeake (*Dodonaea viscosa*), hebes, elaeagnus, mahonia, pyracantha, phormiums and many others will provide effective outer shelter for the vegetable garden. This list is by no means exhaustive, but remember to include a good mix of evergreen varieties amongst the deciduous to ensure year-round shelter. Once an outer framework of shelter is established, the dwarf hedging to enclose the potager may be planted.

Traditional dwarf hedges

'Mock' box (*Lonicera nitida*) For the aspiring potager gardener who has his or her heart set on dwarf hedges and despairs because 400 plants are required, the shrub honeysuckle *Lonicera nitida* makes an extremely acceptable quick-growing substitute for traditional box hedging (*Buxus sempervirens*). The plant bears very dense small leaves and there is an attractive gold variety called 'Baggeson's Gold'. Hardy. Grows easily from cuttings.

English box (*Buxus sempervirens*) is the traditional dwarf hedging for the potager. It is a small shrub with glossy dark green foliage. Height 50 cm (20 in). The variety 'Suffruticosa' (edging box) grows to 25 cm (9 in). The recommended spacing distance for most shrubby hedging plants is 15–20 cm (6–7 in).

Left: This large formal potager is enclosed by a beautifully sculpted hedge of pittosporum, *Pittosporum* 'Karo', trained at the centre into an attractive archway. Bold topiary forms of clipped box combine with the clean lines of the beds to create a potager of strong design and restful simplicity.

Right: Common box, *Buxus sempervirens*, forms the framework for this edible garden and constitutes a strong design feature. The smaller variety *B.* 'Suffruticosa' has been used for dwarf hedgings and edgings.

Above: Young bushes of 'mock box', *Lonicera nitida* 'Baggeson's Gold', enclose this attractive and productive small potager. Growing more quickly than box, lonicera soon forms a neat compact hedge, grows easily from cuttings and is also available in a dark green form.

Taking box or lonicera cuttings for dwarf hedging

The time to take softwood cuttings from box or lonicera is in late summer. Look for strong young shoots that have grown this year. Cut them just above a leaf joint to leave them about 7.5–10 cm (3–4 in) in length.

The best area for rooting on most cuttings is just below a node (leaf joint), so trim the cutting there with a sharp knife. Both box and lonicera cuttings root readily, but a dip into hormone rooting powder will hasten the process. Place the cuttings into a mix of fifty-fifty peat and vermiculite, or three parts sand to one of potting mix. Water well and cover with polythene, then place in the shade. They should root in approximately 8 weeks.

Fruit trees as cordons and espaliers

Since fruit trees are traditionally grown on frames in the potager, as espaliers or cordons, and used as enclosing or dividing elements, I have included the method of training and pruning them to shape within this chapter. The cordon or espalier is a tree which is trained from a single stem to grow flat against a fence or wall.

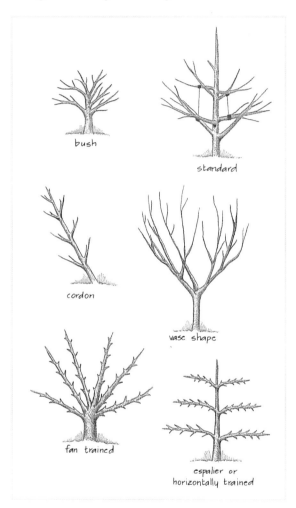

Cordons

Almost all varieties of apples, pears, plums, peaches and nectarines, and many other fruiting trees, can be trained as cordons. Soft fruits such as gooseberry and red and white currants may also be trained in this way. There is a certain apprehension about training fruit trees as cordons and espaliers, but it is not difficult. All that is required is structural support and a well fed, well drained piece of soil in a sunny, sheltered position. For the tiny space potager the single and double cordons are most suitable and simple for the beginner to manage.

Above: Fruit trees trained to cordon or espalier forms on wire frames facilitate easy pruning, spraying and harvesting and allow maximum cropping in a minimal area.

Left: The ancient art of cordon or espalier means training a tree from a single stem to grow flat against a wall or along a wired frame.

Methods for training cordons and espaliers

Posts about 3 m (10 ft) long are driven 65 cm (2 ft 6 in) into the ground and one wire is stretched across, 45 cm (18 in) from the earth. The other two pieces are then stretched across, 65 cm (2 ft 6 in) from each other. The cordons can be planted as close as 45 cm (18 in) apart.

This means one can grow an interesting variety of fruit in a space only 6 m (20 ft) long.

In selecting a suitable fruit-tree sapling, choose a self-fertilising variety. This should be cut back to about 26 cm (10 in) from the ground after planting. Several shoots will then grow out of the stem. All these shoots are removed, except one which is grown to form a rod or single cordon. If you wish to grow a double cordon, then leave one shoot either side of the stem.

The single cordon will have one rod with a number of side shoots or laterals. Pruning is carried out in mid summer when the laterals are cut back to about 15 cm (6 in) from the base. In winter, these shoots are pruned back again to at least three buds. The leader should not be pruned in winter, except to remove the tip to encourage the development of side shoots. The double cordon is pruned the same way as the single cordon.

Another popular cordon or espalier form is the dwarf bush pyramid. This consists of a centre stem with a number of branches extending outward. The bottom branches are 45 cm (18 in) long, and each succeeding branch about 5 cm (2 in) shorter up to the top branches which are 15 cm (6 in) in length. The result will be a dwarf, pyramid-shaped tree. All side shoots are pruned in the same way as the other cordons. No posts or wires are needed. The trees are planted about 1 m (3 ft) apart so that when fully grown the basal branches of each tree will just touch that of its neighbour.

When growing cordons and espaliers, strong supports and shelter from strong winds and hard frosts are essential. Single and double cordons should be planted along a hedge, and the espalier or pyramid against a wall of the house. Like ordinary fruit bushes and trees, cordons are subject to the usual diseases, and winter and summer spraying may be necessary. (See Chapter 8.) The potagist will certainly find the cordon system the best way to grow fruit crops since the method makes it easier to prune, pick and spray the fruit, and requires minimal space.

CHAPTER 4

PLANTING

All vegetables are beautiful, but some are more beautiful than others. Each has its own shape, colour, texture, volume and taste; each evolves over a season into something very different from its point of departure, whether it began as a purchased plant or a seed. In terms of garden design, growing vegetables is largely a kind of foliage gardening, since the leaves of vegetables are infinite in their texture, size and variety and occupy far more space in the potager than their flowers or fruit. Flowers which are not those of the fruiting plants appear in the vegetable garden as companion plants or aromatics, but the basic tapestry is composed of foliage of different

heights and textures, with 'designer veges' strongly featured.

Colour, texture, shape and size

To the casual beholder, almost all vegetables have green leaves and are therefore uninteresting, but if asked to look closely, he or she will observe an enormous range of shapes and textures and variations in all shades of green. Cabbages vary from pale drumheads or ox-hearts to dark glaucous bubbly-leafed savoys. Broad beans stand tall with grey-green leaves and clusters of black and white scented flowers which turn into fat shiny pods. French beans make low mounds of almost heart-shaped mid-green leaves, while runner beans scramble obligingly up supports to flaunt flowers of varying colours. Parsnips and carrots offer delicate feathery plumes, onions and leeks thrust up spears of silvery blue, and block plantings of

Opposite: Red rainbow beet, tomatoes, peppers, courgettes, beans, parsley and dahlias combine colour and texture with vertical accents and lush growth to create this beautifully co-ordinated potager bed.
Above: A block planting of the red lettuce 'Lollo Rossa Foxy' with a lime-green cos variety.

This potager forms a mosaic of colour and scent: the centre of the bed is formed by a planting of red and green lettuces; spring onions throw up tall silver-blue spears to the right of the lettuce and to their rear are plantings of parsley and white-ribbed Chinese cabbage bok choy. Borage flowers create a haze of blue and the colours are vibrant and warm in the exciting bed to the rear, which is enclosed with old roses underplanted with red bergamot, bronze fennel, red orache, red astilbes, red sage, red rainbow beet, red lettuce and nasturtiums.

potatoes offer foliage of dark rich green relieved by masses of white or purple flowers.

Colour

Once one starts studying edible plants for their beauty as well as their productivity, the desire to experiment with exciting new designer veg (in addition to traditional varieties) is born. One realises there is as much scope for experimenting with colour in the potager as there is in the flower borders. A gentle blending of colour, for example, would be a row of butterhead lettuces unfolding soft green leaves from a paler heart in juxtaposition with a row of stiff-leaved cabbages with purple-red veinings on bold silvery-blue leaves. A bed offering great contrast of foliage form, texture and colour might incorporate informal plantings of globe artichokes, frilly oak-leaved lettuces of red and green, and clumps of bush or dwarf beans with heart-shaped leaves and flowers of varying colours.

A planting combination offering bold colour might incorporate rows of tagetes (marigolds) and rows of a modern hybrid beet-root which has foliage of glossy green, heavily tinged and veined with purplish-red. Gold and bronze climbing nasturtiums could be set to scramble up a tepee of climbing beans with bright coral flowers. In English and European potagers brilliant flowers such as dahlias (especially the hybrids with stunning purple-black leaves) or zinnias are used to provide visual excitement and contrast to the darker green of leafy vegetables.

Shades of silver

The globe artichoke and its near relative, the cardoon, offer restful tones of silver in addition to dramatic felted foliage. For striking variance of colour, form and texture group the latter with white cosmos and border these with clumps of cool blue lavenders – a planting combination bees and beneficial insects also find irresistible.

Variegation for contrast

Edible plants offering the contrast of variegated leaves include some cucurbits with dark green foliage dappled with greyish-white, and herbs such as mint, marjoram and lemon balm. The variegated sages are particularly attractive, coming in gold (var. 'Icterina') or deep green splashed with gold. Common sage (*Salvia officinalis*) offers dark grey-green leaves with rosy-purple overtones, and there is a delightful cultivar bearing cream and green foliage with purple-pink overtones.

The nasturtium cultivar 'Alaska' offers foliage marbled cream. Other vegetables in this category, while not strictly variegated but having stems which are markedly different from their leaves, include golden celery, the Chinese brassicas, kohlrabi (which comes in two colours – white stems with pale green leaves, or with silvery foliage tinged pink above rosy-purple stems and bulb), beetroot with reddish stems and deep green leaves veined wine-red, and of course, the glowing rainbow chards.

An eyecatching onion is the popular red bunching variety (*Allium fistulosum*) which is grown and used in the same way as spring onions but has glowing red stalks which add pizazz to any salad or culinary display.

A planting combination offering a delightful juxtaposition of colour, texture and form is a border of wine-red ruby chard backed by the silver spears of leeks.

With the exception of the amaranth species and rainbow chard, garnet-red edible plants are rare, but there are several offering purple-red tones – the tall red orache, red Brussels sprouts, the yellow-flowered but purple-stemmed oriental mustard, the radicchio chicories, the darker beetroots (of which 'Bull's Blood' is the darkest), aromatic reddish-purple perilla and several basil cultivars (see page 79).

The choice of red-tinged and green-bronze ornamental lettuces is now extensive, some having oak-shaped leaves and others attractively ruffled. They are so aesthetically pleasing that they are used as border plants or quick fillers,

Regarded as a dietary staple for many centuries, the humble cabbage is humble no more. A block planting of winter savoy hybrids with magnificent silver-purple leaves are set off to perfection by clipped hedges of golden-tipped box and balls of privet.

and make particularly colourful plant association with vegetables of solid reds.

The key to successful colour permutations in the potager is happy experimentation. A glance at a seedsman's catalogue or the shelves of any good garden centre reveals that the exciting range of designer veg and herbs at our disposal is greater than ever before. Our concern here is not with extensive lists of hybrid names, but with a basic guide to traditional stalwarts suitable for potager cultivation. The fact that each might now be on offer in any number of different guises is a bonus which will lead the potagist on a voyage of (edible) discovery!

The Quick Reference Guide in Chapter 7 gives additional details on the life cycle, size, colour, and siting of edible plants through vegetables, fruit and nuts.

General management in the potager: continuity of produce and catch crops

There are a number of ways to maximise the yields from your potager and ensure a steady continuity of produce.

1. Maintain such a high state of soil fertility with regular dressings of compost, organic materials, natural plant foods and manure that plants can be grown at the greatest possible density. Detailed information on fertilisers is given in Chapter 6.
2. Spread the growing season over as long a period as possible by sowing early, middle and late varieties. Your nurseryman will recommend appropriate cultivars.
3. If you cannot run to a greenhouse, build a basic cold frame as detailed in Chapter 6. Fill it with your own seedlings in pots so that you always have replacement plants for those that have cropped. Harden them off in a sunny sheltered corner before planting out. Protect early season seedlings with the polythene cloches also described in Chapter 6.
4. Make successive sowings of each crop rather than one huge one for sustained yield. Glut is fine if you have time for and enjoy

freezing, jamming, juicing, saucing, pickling and puréeing. The culinary possibilities of the contents of your potager all maturing at once are limited and your family may not appreciate becoming vegetarian slave labourers who own a dozen chest freezers!
5. Interplant larger, slow-to-mature vegetables with catch crops.

'Catch crops' are smaller, quick-to-mature vegetables such as salad stuffs, oriental vegetables, dwarf beans, etc., which may be planted under or between larger vegetables and utilised as 'fillers'. They maximise potager soil space and help prevent weed formation.

Vegetable stalwarts and gourmet delights

The list of vegetable varieties below is by no means exhaustive but noted are cultivars for which seeds are obtainable from nurserymen worldwide where geographical location and climatic conditions permit their cultivation. In most cases the plants will be available as seedlings in punnets from all good garden centres.

Asparagus *(Asparagus officinalis)*

The French philosopher and playwright Marcel Proust was overcome by the beauty of asparagus tips and describes his delight thus:

a vegetable dipped in pink and ultramarine, spikes delicately daubed with mauve and azure changing colour little by little down to their feet . . . with iridescences that are not of this world . . .

Art of French Vegetable Gardening, Louisa Jones (full details in bibliography)

He was doubtless aware that it was also exceptionally good to eat!

This Southern European plant is a long-lived perennial cultivated for its rich succulent tips. Many gardeners are put off growing asparagus because it usually takes three or more years from planting until the first crop, and its fruiting

season is brief. However, if one has the room it is a rewarding plant because it can remain in the same ground for many years, and few plants are more decorative during summer and autumn when its strong green plumes gradually turn to butter gold. (It looks marvellous with vibrant dark coral nasturtiums.) A small plot will give great pleasure in spring when the fat new tips appear, but the bed does have the disadvantage of having to be kept weed free for long periods. The sowing of various green manure cover crops is the best remedy – phacelia, salad greens or pot marigolds are most beneficial and smother weeds.

Asparagus requires a well drained moderately fertile soil. Start by buying one- or two-year-old crowns and setting them out 45 cm (18 in) apart in a well prepared trench and wait two

Block plantings of potatoes in front, broccoli and beet in the middle and broad beans to the rear fill the beds of this healthy and productive potager. The prolific rich red rose 'Dublin Bay', underplanted with cucurbits and catmint, the white walls and striped blinds of the cottage combine to create an attractive setting for the vegetable beds.

years for the first crop. Alternatively, sow all male F1 hybrid seeds and start them in pots before moving them out to a raised bed. These will yield a small harvest during the second summer. Properly cared for and not over-cropped, this vegetable for the gourmet gardener will produce more and more shoots for 10 to 20 years, so do give it potager space if you can. 'Lucullus' is an excellent proven cropper. 'Franklin' produces thicker spears and a heavier crop.

Asparagus pea *(Tetragonolobus purpureus)*
A fast growing and cropping member of the legume family but neither asparagus nor true pea, this small vetch-like plant has attractive red flowers and tasty winged pods. Harvested young, the pods steamed and served with a knob of butter combine the flavours of both peas and asparagus. A native of the Mediterranean, asparagus pea is frost tender so should be sown indoors and planted out in late spring. If sown straight into the garden set seeds 2 cm (¼ in) deep in rows 30–40 cm (12–15 in) apart. Asparagus pea will grow to about 45 cm (18 in) tall if supported and will spread to 60 cm (2 ft). Requires a light rich soil and a sunny position. Harvested regularly, it will crop over a long period.

Aubergines or eggplants *(Solanum melongena)*
A beautiful tropical and subtropical vegetable which has been grown in China for nearly 3000 years, the aubergine/eggplant in cooler climates requires greenhouse or container cultivation but in warmer areas will do well in any sunny sheltered corner. The plant rarely exceeds 1 m (3 ft) and the main tips should be pinched out to encourage bushy growth. There are many varieties of aubergines/eggplants with whitish egg-shaped fruit but they are less productive than the more familiar polished purple-black varieties.

The plants and the fruit of Japanese hybrids are smaller, but mature earlier and are prolific yielders, often bearing 40–50 fruit per stem. An international and highly decorative favourite is 'Florence Round Purple' or 'Violetta de Firenze', an eggplant with oblong to round fruits in shades of lavender often striped with creamy-white. This cultivar has the added virtue of being tolerant of less than perfect conditions. Aubergine 'Easter Egg' is an early cropping variety with oval-shaped white satin-skinned fruit which is excellent for container growing.

Aubergines require a loose, well drained soil, rich but slightly acid, and consistently warm temperatures. Cultivars over 45 cm (18 in) tall will need staking and plants should be well watered to avoid leaf and bud fall.

The eggplant is a beautiful vegetable, its midnight black glossy fruit adding dramatic colour and accents among other vegetable crops. It is also attractive in bloom, bearing dark lilac-purple flowers, and some varieties have purple stems. A grouping of three varieties of mixed colours will make a stunning corner or centrepiece for a courtyard or container garden. Aubergines should be picked when young and are excellent for frying, pickling and many other culinary uses.

Beans
This most useful vegetable was brought to Europe by the Spanish in the sixteenth century. The genus is highly decorative because beans come in an infinite range of colours, shapes and sizes, and some varieties have patterned skins.

Beans may be sown in peat pots in spring but should not be planted out until warm weather is assured. Recommended spacing for bush beans is 16 cm (6 in) apart, but they do equally well 10 cm (4 in) apart and cover the soil with a moisture-retaining canopy of foliage. All beans like well manured, moisture-retaining soil. Avoid fertilisers with heavy nitrogen content because this will promote lush foliage at the expense of flowers. Beans themselves are a valuable crop for fixing nitrogen in the soil.

All varieties of beans need constant harvesting for continual cropping. They are prone to black and white fly infestation, so plant feverfew with early varieties and nasturtiums with late varieties to divert these pests.

Dwarf or bush beans *(Phaseolus vulgaris)*
These bush plants, grown for tiny fresh beans, make good fillers, and can be dotted about the potager in clumps since they enrich the soil and mature fast. Among the bush varieties, the yellow butter beans and the purple-podded varieties are both delicious and decorative.

Runner or climbing beans *(P. multiflorus, P.*

coccineus) are among the most prolific and easily grown of all vegetable crops. Grown on tepees of wooden or bamboo stakes, they make strong vertical accents in the potager and provide vivid colour with attractive flowers ranging from deep scarlet, coral red, lavender or white, depending on the variety.

Broad beans (*Vicia faba*) are a hardy old European native providing nourishing protein-packed food and green waste for the compost heap. Nitrogen compounds are made by bacteria in the roots, which are released to the next crop when the tops are cut off. A useful vegetable for sowing straight into the soil in late autumn in warmer areas to overwinter, but in the coldest areas best sown in pots in the greenhouse for planting out when soils are warmer. The long pod varieties, with eight to ten beans per pod, are tall – 1.2 m (3 ft 3 in) and need support. 'Exhibiton Longpod' and 'Sutton's Green' are tried and tested stalwarts. Taller varieties should have their tips pinched out at 1 m (3 ft) to prevent them becoming leggy and to promote more flowers. The shorter-podded variety 'Windsor' can be tall or dwarf, and a popular variety offering compact growth for small spaces is 'The Sutton', growing to just over 30 cm (1 ft) high. Cultivation requirements are the same as for other bean varieties.

Beetroot (*Beta vulgaris*)

A European native, beetroot is closely related to sugarbeet. Both standard and globe varieties come in a range of exciting colours and shapes, but the most decorative for the potager are the old-fashioned wine-red varieties such as 'Bull's Blood' with claret-tinged foliage. Many of the traditional stalwarts have highly decorative rich green foliage tinged crimson above garnet globes; others have green leaves, pink stems and globes ringed with white, and newer varieties offer both white and gold fruit which do not 'bleed' and create an attractive contrast in both salads or cooked vegetable dishes – a veritable rainbow of beetroots!

Beetroot are patient vegetables which can remain in the ground for some time before they get woody or past their prime. In all but the coldest months of the year they make a beautiful combination mixed with dwarf nasturtiums or the silvery spears of leeks. Favourites for containers or small beds are varieties of the baby beets. Their sweet-flavoured miniature globes make them universally popular as gourmet baby vegetables.

Start beetroot seeds in pots in early spring, or sow out of doors in early summer about 5 cm (2 in) apart. Seed will not germinate at temperatures lower than 7°C (45°F). There is no need to thin the seedlings, they will simply push each other out of the way to form excellent young baby beet. Because of their decorative value beetrot crops make excellent borders. They require well drained but moist, light soil, with high nitrogen levels and plenty of humus but no fresh manure.

Beet – Swiss chard (*Beta vulgaris* var. *cicla*)

Swiss chard or silverbeet is a highly decorative, hardy member of the beet family which withstands heat and drought better than other vegetables and will tolerate some shade. Its vertical growth habit makes an excellent small-space crop. The bright translucent wine-red or golden stems positively glow in the sun in contrast to the topping of dark green bubbly foliage, which is rich in vitamins and may be used as a salad and spinach-type vegetable. The leaves should be harvested young on a 'cut and come again' principle. A universally popular beet variety is 'Tricolour' which is a beautiful mixture of chard (silverbeet), with stems of gold, red and white. At maturity reaching about 60 cm (2 ft), these rainbow beet make exciting colour contrasts in the potager and are so ornamental that they are often grown in the flower bed, or not harvested at all!

Beets will cope with container cultivation and a wide range of soils. Like beetroot, each 'seed' is a cluster of seeds and the weakest can be nipped out to leave the strongest seedlings.

Broccoli (*Brassica oleracea* subvar. *botrytis* var. *cymosa*)

In addition to being good to eat and chock-full of iron and vitamins, broccoli has become highly decorative. The spiral-coned lime-green heads of the popular variety 'Romanesco', piled up like layers of tiny seashells, or the little red mushrooms of the purple, cut-and-come-again varieties are both a culinary and visual delight. The foliage of most broccoli is an attractive silvery-green with pale midribs. Purple-sprouting and white-sprouting varieties make large spreading plants up to 1 m (3 ft) high which may need staking. The plants take up to 45 weeks to mature from sowing, but since much of this time is over winter, they are well worth their space for groundcover and early cropping in spring.

The planting of various traditional varieties will allow harvesting over long periods. For the earliest crop of the **Calabrese broccoli** use stalwarts such as 'Mercedes', followed by 'Corvet', and late in the season plant 'White or Purple Sprouting', which will crop throughout winter and spring in all but the coldest regions.

The widely obtainable dwarf 'Brocoletto Raab' grows to just 24 cm (8 in), making an ideal catch crop since it matures in 6–8 weeks. Sow directly into the soil, scatter in small clumps, or use as an underplanting beneath taller vegetables of vertical growth habit. This most versatile variety combines the best of mustard greens and broccoli for salads and stir-fries. Always pick the central stem of any mature broccoli plant first to encourage side-heads to develop for prolonged cropping.

Brussels sprouts (*Brassica oleracea bullata* subvar. *gemmifera*)

As a general rule sprouts take 28–36 weeks to mature, depending on the variety, and stand between 45 cm (18 in) and 1 m (3 ft) in height. The most decorative of the traditional sprout family is the attractive red 'Rubine' which is shorter and better looking than the green vari-

eties and has a more refined flavour. Green-balled 'Montgomery' grows up to 1 m (3 ft) and crops well. In windy positions the roots of the sprout must be in firm soil and may need staking since plants are susceptible to wind-rock. Cultivation requirements are much the same as for broccoli.

Cabbage (*Brassica oleracea* subvar. *capitata*)

The cabbage is humble no longer. This erstwhile dietary staple has entered the ranks of designer veg, offering a wide variety of heights and volumes as well as colours. It is one of the most decorative plant families for year-round productivity and visual appeal. Cabbages come in every shape and size imaginable – pale green and smooth, crinkly-leafed and dark blue-green, or in wonderful garnet reds which enliven the potager and add colour contrast among other edible plants at any time of the year.

Young cabbages can be underplanted with catch crops such as radish, lettuce, or spring onions which mature quickly, or with flowering companion plants. Cabbage have long been grown in rows but have far greater visual impact if grown in blocks, an added advantage being that one is able to crop from around the outer edges, thereby avoiding a glaring snag-toothed gap when a head is removed from a row! This is particularly important in the small-space potager where limited ground allows groups of only four to six. Cabbages look particularly attractive edged with dwarf marigolds.

The average cabbage stands 37–45 cm (14–18 in) high and spreads to 45 cm (18 in). Spring cabbages generally have conical or 'ox-heart' heads. They overwinter from mid-to-late summer sowing, taking about 30–40 weeks to mature. Summer and winter cabbages are generally round-headed and are smooth-leaved. Late autumn and winter varieties tend towards darker colours and less smooth leaves but this category also includes the white cabbages used for coleslaw. Both take between 20 to 35 weeks to mature. For harsh winter conditions, the traditional variety 'Tundra' is one of the hardiest, and an easily obtainable stunning red cabbage to provide welcome winter colour is 'Ruby Ball' which makes a perfect foil to the silvery crinkled leaves of the hearty savoys, which are also winter varieties. They are dark green, with deeply puckered bubbly leaves, while red cabbages are fairly smooth and a deep purply-red colour with a beautiful bloom on both sides of the leaves. Another universally popular deep-red cabbage is 'Rookie', its mature head weighing some 2 kg (4½ lbs). The rich colour of red cabbages makes them valuable decorative additions to the potager and in the kitchen, where they look most inviting in almost any dish.

The cultivation requirements of the traditional European-type cabbage family is much the same as for broccoli and sprouts, except that cabbages need controlled watering if the weather is dry. A sudden drenching can cause the heads to split, which leads to deterioration of the flesh. It is wise to stagger plantings of cabbage to avoid them all maturing at the same time – the culinary possibilities with a whole bed of cabbages are limited! Wider spacing between cabbages produces bigger heads, but picked younger and smaller, their taste is much sweeter.

Chinese cabbages (*Brassica rapa* subvar. *pekinensis* and *chinenses*)

The flavour of versatile oriental cabbage hybrids is more delicate than that of traditional European varieties, their leaves are usually far crisper and they mature far more quickly. Picked young and shredded finely and tossed in ginger, soy sauce, sesame seed and a little rice-wine vinegar, they make deliciously crunchy stir-fries, salads or coleslaws. Most varieties can be sown almost year round in most areas, plants growing erect in warm temperatures but showing a more prostrate habit in cooler conditions where they are remarkably cold hardy.

Chinese cabbages come in many decorative and delicious forms. The traditional 'Two Seasons' variety crops from both early spring

Savoy cabbages with handsome silver-blue leaves create a visually pleasing block planting. The bed to the right is planted with a pattern of young cauliflowers, the red lettuce 'Quatre Saisons' and shallots.

and summer-autumn sowings. Although a highly productive crop, it takes little space, having large oval heads 25 x 18 cm (9 x 7 in) with thick succulent midribs and crisp, tender, tightly savoyed leaves. The **pak choi** hybrids are quite different in form and are widely grown for their crisp single-flower-topped stalks of green or purplish-red. The huge range of oriental brassicas now freely available offer the potagist an immense variety of shape, form, size, colour and flavour. There is also a delightful range of dwarf hybrids. The Chinese brassicas do not transplant well and are best sown into seed beds or into peat pots which may be put straight into the soil without root disturbance. They require rich well drained soil in full sun and regular watering.

There are many other excellent Chinese greens. Please refer to the Quick Reference Guide, Chapter 7, for a full list of other hybrids and oriental vegetables.

Capsicum and chilli peppers *(Capsicum annum)*

Hot or chilli peppers and sweet peppers are botanically identical and can be grown out of doors in warm areas. F1 hybrids are available for cooler climates with shorter summers. These highly decorative plants, treasured for their pungent, aromatic fruit, compact bushy growth and prolific fruiting, in addition to their aesthetic appeal, enjoy a demand which has resulted in many varieties of both sweet and chilli peppers being available to home growers and gardeners. Chilli and sweet pepper plants originated from Central America and Mexico and make glossy-leaved bushes up to 1.2 m (3 ft 3 in) tall, depending on the variety, and are now used around the world for international cuisine.

Many people believe chilli peppers exist only to make food so hot that all other flavour is obliterated – a sadly incorrect perception since many hybrids are sweet and juicy and have no heat at all.

These attractive plants mostly have small white blossoms and many varieties of peppers start green and ripen to their final colour. Sweet pepper hybrids are available in red, purple, orange or gold, and more modern introductions are 'tomato peppers', which form medium-sized bushes bearing prolific crops of thick-walled, juicy fruit which is delicious cooked or raw. Most of the chilli varieties also ripen from green to red, and varieties are available with fruits varying from long and thin to short and fat.

Bell and sweet peppers are one of the most traditionally cultivated sweet varieties with thick-walled green fruits which are about 12 cm (5 in) long and turn to red as they mature. A universal favourite is 'California Wonder – Golden' which has all the virtues of the green-red pepper but turns a rich golden yellow at maturity. Plants grow to 60 cm (2 ft) high. They have a sweet crisp flavour and are excellent for stuffing, frying or eating raw.

Hot chillies and peppers in all parts of their plants carry the oils that give the heat which will damage sensitive human skin tissue, so be sure to wash your hands well after handling the seeds or plants, especially before touching the eyes or nose.

A good tip for skinning chilli peppers is to place them under a preheated grill and turn frequently until the skins are blistered and can be peeled off. There are many highly decorative and delicious chilli pepper varieties, ranging from the fiery hot traditional 'Habanero', 'Tabasco', 'Serrano' and 'Jalapeno' hybrids, through those of medium heat like 'Anaheim' and 'Cayenne', to the spicier sweeter fruits of 'Poblano', 'Mulato' and 'Numex Sweet' hybrids.

Peppers need warm fertile soil with good drainage and full sun. They make excellent container subjects in cooler climates, where they may be moved into sunny sheltered positions to make attractive focal points or features. Peppers have a small root ball and are best sown first in peat pots so that they can be transplanted without root disturbance when the soil is consistently warm.

Cardoon *(Cynara cardunculus)*

This handsome architectural Mediterranean native is of immense value in the potager, both for its aesthetic and culinary benefits.

Cardoon is a tall plant growing some 2 m (7 ft) high. It has giant leaves of deeply dissected silvery-green, and spectacular lavender thistle-like flowers.

The plant's thick white stalks are blanched and eaten in sauces or like celery. If not allowed to flower the globe heads can also be eaten like those of the globe artichoke. Like the latter, the cardoon is a perennial and reproduces itself by offshoots as well as seeds. The traditional variety, 'White Ivory', is the best edible hybrid.

Sow cardoon seeds in pots and plant out of doors in late spring, allowing 1 m (3 ft) spacing between plants. Dress with manure or compost in winter and do not allow cardoons to flower if you want to blanch the stems for eating.

Carrots (*Daucus carota*)

Carrots lend themselves very well to interplanting with onions and leeks, which help protect them from carrot fly. A row of mature carrots provides a stream of delicate fern-like foliage which makes a beautiful border and an excellent foil for the bolder foliage of brassicas and cucurbits. These stalwarts of the vegetable plot contain beta-carotene, which assists the body to manufacture Vitamin A to help ward off heart attacks and strokes, and to discourage the formation of artery-clogging cholesterol.

Planting traditional varieties such as early 'Rondo', which has round roots, followed by mid season 'Nantes' and then late 'Berlicum-Berjo', gives a prolonged season of cropping. Popular modern varieties include the dwarf carrots with flavoursome globe-shaped roots – favourites with restaurants and gourmet gardeners as 'baby vegetables'.

Carrot seed is slow to germinate and needs a little patience. The crop requires stone-free, very loose, free-draining soil with low nitrogen levels. With the exception of the round-rooted varieties, they are best sown straight into the soil.

Cauliflower (*Brassica oleracea* subvar. *botrytis*)

Originating from the eastern Mediterranean, cauliflowers were a vegetable much admired by the Romans. Modern summer varieties take about 20 weeks to mature and winter varieties 40–50 weeks, but this is a vegetable well worth growing because there are now varieties which permit year-round cropping.

Cauliflowers, like cabbages, look best grown in blocks so that harvesting can take place from around the outer edges, avoiding an eyecatching gap in the middle of a row. Ideally the heads or curds of the white varieties should be covered over with the adjacent leaves for protection, which does minimise their visual impact.

The traditional creamy-white-headed varieties, though highly attractive in themselves, are now rivalled by hybrids with purple or lime-green florets. An exciting variety effected by the surprise marriage of the broccoli and the cauliflower has resulted in the delightful modern hybrid 'Alverda', called a **broccoflower**, which combines the flavour of both parents! This unique open-pollinated combination prefers the cool, even growing conditions of spring or autumn. For the small potager, universally available dwarf cauliflower hybrids include 'Alpha' (syn. 'Polaris') and 'Idol'. A traditional purple variety is 'Violet Queen' with rich rosy-violet florets that are fine in texture and have a high mineral content, that accounts for its colour. Easy to grow, it loses some colour on cooking, but the violet florets, broken up into small pieces, lend wonderful accents and contrasts to salads and other cold dishes.

Cauliflower plants should be spaced out in groups a minimum of 60 cm (2 ft) apart because they mature to big vegetables. They require fertile soil and plenty of water to prevent bolting. Winter varieties will benefit from a dressing of good homemade compost or blood, fish and bone meal. Like other brassicas, cauliflowers suffer from clubroot disease, so plantings need to be strictly rotated to avoid a build-up of disease spores in the soil.

Celeriac (*Apium graveolens* var. *rapaceum*)

Celeriac is cultivated for its swollen stem rather than its leaves or stalk, which are not considered edible. It makes a delicious vegetable either grated raw in salads or cooked. A European native, celeriac is identical botanically to celery, and is often referred to as turnip-rooted celery. It makes a bushy plant about 45 cm (18 in) high, with dark green leaves identical to those of celery. Young plants should be spaced 30 cm (1 ft) apart, but the leaves become too dense to allow catch cropping with anything slower to mature than radishes. The lower leaves should be removed regularly to encourage the bulb of the stem to mature. Traditional recommended varieties include 'Snow White' and ' Tellus'.

Celery *(Apium graveolens)*

The best celeries for the potager are the hardy 'self-blanching' varieties which may be grown in close blocks that exclude the light from the stems. Ideally the stems should be wrapped but intercropping between taller vegetables achieves this light exclusion just as well. Of the self-blanching varieties the traditional 'Celebrity' is best, producing long crisp stems which will even stand a little frost.

Chinese celeries of the 'Kunn Choi' varieties have virtually the same form as normal celery but differ in size, have a more pronounced flavour, and are well suited to the potager because they mature in just over half the time of traditional varieties. The stalks are roundish and seldom measure more than 1.5 cm ($^1/_2$ in) in diameter or more than 23 cm (8 in) in length. Plants may be also be grown out of doors in pots for a year-round supply. If sown direct into the soil or a container, plant the seeds thickly, approximately 6 mm ($^1/_8$ in) deep and transplant when 10–12 cm (4–5 in) high to approximately 30 cm (1 ft) apart.

The celery family requires a sunny position in moist, well manured soil with regular watering in dry weather to prevent them flowering, seeding and bolting prematurely, before the stalks (or as in the case of celeriac, see below, the swollen stem base) are ready for eating.

Chicory and endive *(Cichorium intybus, C. endivia)*

Both chicory and endive are used in salads and resemble lettuce. Endive has a loose heart, whereas chicory leaves are larger and the heart is more compact. Chicory is blanched (to remove the bitter taste) by covering with pots, straw or black polythene for two to three weeks before harvesting. It is then called witloof.

Another variety of chicory, beloved of potagists, is the highly ornamental cabbage-shaped red radicchio hybrids which mature to give colour in winter. They do not require blanching. Chicory and endive hybrids look wonderful towards the front of a border, and the green varieties, if allowed to seed, bear striking daisy flowers of intense blue. Other ornamental varieties come with green foliage splashed with red or red stroked with white.

Endive (*Cichorium endivia*) is a close cousin of chicory and cultivated in the same way. It comes in two forms – broad-leaved which looks much like a loose-leaf lettuce, and the bright light-green curly-leafed type which provides exciting textural contrast in the garden.

Chicories are tolerant of a wide range of soils. They have a tendency to bolt if sown in low temperatures, so wait until early summer for the green varieties and mid-to-late summer for the red varieties.

Courgette (zucchini) *(Cucurbita pepo ovifera)*

Courgettes or zucchinis are baby bush marrows, but the varieties sold as courgettes have been selected for tender skin, good flavour and heavy cropping. Spreading up to 1.2 m (3 ft 3 in) wide and growing 1 m (3 ft) high, they make handsome plants with silvery-green deeply cut leaves borne on prickly stems. Huge edible golden chalice flowers turn into shiny fruit which may be dark or mid-green, golden yellow or almost white. The golden-fruited hybrids such as 'Golden Zucchini' are particularly attractive since they also have yellowish leaves, which help brighten dark corners.

Originating from tropical areas of America, courgettes are frost tender and require warm rich soils and frequent watering.

Cress

Land cress (*Barbarea verna*) is an easily grown vegetable much like watercress and is sold simply as 'land cress', 'winter cress' or 'American cress'. Best sown in two patches near the front of a border in rows 15 cm (6 in) apart, the first in early spring for summer use and again in autumn for winter use. Tolerant of varied soils but requires moisture.

This larger potager features a variety of vegetables. Edged with parsley, the front bed features beetroot, red lettuce and carrots and a deep border of the edible marigold *Calendula officinalis*, backed by parsley and nasturtiums. Beds to the left contain onions, spring onions and young dwarf beans. Those to the right, bordered by chives, feature rows of the handsome dark red beetroot 'Bulls Blood'.

Fennel, Florence or Florentine (finnochio)

Grown as a vegetable rich in vitamins, **Florence fennel** (*Foeniculum vulgare* var. *azoricum*) is both versatile and beautiful. Although closely related to the perennial herb fennel, this variety is tender and grown as an annual for its bulbous stems. Standing about 45 cm (18 in) high, it has a fan of light green fern-like foliage. Its pale green pseudo-bulb has an unusual and distinctive flavour, rather like an anise-flavoured celery. Formed by a number of broad whitish sheaths swollen at the stem base, the 'bulb' is partly visible above the soil and sends up delicate feathery foliage much like that of dill. Florence fennel or finnochio, an annual, is not to be confused with common fennel, the perennial which is grown more as a herb for its richly redolent stalks and seeds, and sometimes purely for its highly decorative tall stems bearing filmy reddish-bronze plumes (see page 80).

Garlic (Allium sativum)

The foliage of this odiferous but indispensable herb looks much like that of onions while growing, and harvested fresh from the garden has an incomparable flavour. In addition to its culinary purposes, garlic is extensively used as a companion plant and utilised as an organic spray to repel insects. It is planted as an annual by detaching bulblets from the parent clove and requires a position of full sun and well drained soil.

There are now many varieties of garlic. The following are popular, well tried and tested varieties: **Chinese garlic** – strong flavour; **elephant garlic** – large juicy cloves of mild flavour; **Italian garlic** – red-skinned and easy to peel, rich medium flavour. The variety 'Printanor' has large cloves of mild flavour. (See also page 80.)

Globe artichoke *(Cynara scolymus)*

This gourmet's delight is a native of the Mediterranean but, grown in a position of full sun, adapts well to cooler climates. The plant requires plenty of space since its dramatic deeply dissected silver leaves grow up to 1 m (3 ft) high and its flower stalks can reach up to 1.5 m (5 ft). The attractive flowerheads, which have pretty bracts of silver-green, tinged lavender, require picking while still closed for the tenderest flesh.

Artichokes are easily raised from seed, one to a pot, and since they are gross feeders require moist well manured soil. Universally popular varieties include 'Vert de Laon' and the traditional 'Green Globe'. (See also page 88.)

Jerusalem artichoke *(Helianthus tuberosus)*

In truth this tall handsome plant (sometimes also called a 'sunchoke') is neither an artichoke nor from Jerusalem – it is a sunflower which forms plump tubers and originates from North America! It requires hot summers to produce its bold golden blooms, which follow the arc of the sun. This may account for its name from a corruption of the Italian *girasole* – loosely translated, 'circle the sun'. But the artichoke bit still remains a mystery.

The plants reach 2.4 m (approximately 8 ft) in height and provide an excellent if temporary screen or backdrop in the potager. They have hairy green leaves and tough stems and are a thirsty species so it is best not to plant other edibles too close to their tubers. In very windy areas it may be necessary to heap the earth up or place stones around their roots to give stability. Although Jerusalem artichokes will grow easily from the peelings of a previous crop, the crop yield is in direct proportion to the size of the tuber planted, so if they are a favourite vegetable, try to plant full-sized tubers 30 cm (1 ft) apart in any reasonably fertile but moist soil.

It is important to remove all the tubers at the end of the season because they will quickly reproduce to form a dense clump. The tubers may have red or white skin, but the flesh is always white. The red-skinned varieties are less knobbly to peel and have a slightly better flavour.

Kale *(Brassica oleracea var. acephala)*

This hitherto despised edible has reached the ranks of designer veg! Enormously versatile, the modern kales with their nuances of red, green, cream, pink and purple must be among the most dramatic of all ornamental vegetables. They are particularly prized during long dreary winter months for their cheerful and extravagant colour combinations. Low growing and compact, they are particularly effective in block plantings and as temporary borders where their froths of pink, purple and cream among the green are inherently strong in structure and subtle in colour.

It is important that kale leaves are picked young for both salads and cooked vegetable dishes. For the latter, the young leaves are excellent sprinkled with a little soy sauce and fresh crushed ginger and lightly steamed. The older leaves are invaluable for decorative purposes – they make stunning 'plates' for salads, cold meats, fish, cheeses and many other dishes.

The potagist has a wealth of colourful kale hybrids at his or her disposal, and some varieties come with finely dissected elongated foliage which is highly decorative. Kales are regarded as a winter vegetable and cultivation requirements are the same as those for the brassica family.

Kohlrabi *(Brassica oleracea var. gongylodes)*

Kohlrabi is classified as a root vegetable, but it is the swollen base of the stem which is eaten. White-stemmed with light green leaves and white bulb, or purple-stemmed with purple-tinged leaves and purple bulb, kohlrabi make amusing little plants which resemble sputniks. Enjoying the same conditions as brassicas, they provide an attractive edging for a bed of cabbages either in the same colour or as a foil to different colours. The bulbs, which should be harvested young, have a delicate nutty flavour and may be steamed or roasted, or added to stir-fries and soups. Chopped finely, they make colourful and unusual raw additions to salads.

Leeks (Allium porrum)

There are records dating back to 3200 BC of leeks growing in ancient Egypt. A cold-hardy traditional winter vegetable with a fine mild onion flavour, some varieties have highly decorative violet-blue upright spears which provide an elegant foil for looser-leafed crops. The French variety 'St Victor' is the traditional favourite among the blue varieties.

Leeks are easily germinated from seed and though they require garden space over a number of months, their striking vertical stalks add strength to the overall potager design, and may be interplanted with catch crops such as salad stuffs and beetroot or borders of flowers. Leeks, like onions, are often interplanted with carrots for mutual protection against insects and to utilise all available ground space. The crop requires well drained, rich, loose soil. The latter is essential if you intend to earth up soil around the white stems to blanch them. An alternative is to sow the seeds thickly and blanch by mulching deeply with compost as the plants grow.

Lettuce (Lactuca sativa)

Lettuces are now among the most decorative of garden vegetables and often used in the potager as edgers, left to grow tall and run to seed or employed in alternate blocks of colour to give patchwork and chequered effects. Exciting **Italian and American red varieties** such as 'Lollo Rosso', 'Casablanca', 'Salad Bowl', 'Lovina', 'Merveille de Quatre Saisons' and 'Rouge d'Hiver' are now available in many countries. **Green cultivars** include 'Green Ice', 'Royal Oak Leaf' with rich dark leaves, 'Tango' with deeply cut pointed leaves like endive, 'Lollo Biondo' with ruffled leaves, and the butterhead varieties with smooth foliage of soft pale green. An additional virtue of modern hybrids such as these is that many have been bred for a 'cut and come again' cropping. One plant will give sustained yield if the leaves are frequently harvested. A **gourmet dwarf variety** beloved of chefs is the baby cos lettuce 'Little Gem' which grows to 15 cm (6 in) and has tightly folded dark upright heads.

With careful timing and choice of varieties it is now possible in all but the coldest areas to have lettuce all year round. They require frequent watering in warmer months to prevent bolting.

Marrows, squashes, pumpkins and cucumbers

The fruit and foliage of the cucurbit family is among the most prolific and highly decorative of all vegetables. The family is extensive and includes cucumbers, squash, pumpkin and melons which give their bounty from mid summer to late autumn. When the large bold foliage develops it covers a lot of ground, but cucurbits look marvellous when grown vertically on trellises, frames or archways. The hanging fruit, viewed at eye level instead of hidden beneath large leaves, makes a delightfully bold and decorative feature in the potager.

An attractive idea, particularly in the small-space garden, is to plant cucurbits in large terracotta pots placed at intervals on top of a medium-height wall (for easy watering). The stems bearing fruit and golden chalice flowers make a most attractive focal point at eye level and leave the ground free for vegetables of a more terrestrial nature. The developing fruits should be exposed to the sun by the careful cutting back of old foliage. If the crops are being grown at ground level this may be achieved by lifting the developing fruits onto a couple of old bricks, tiles or flat stones.

Marrows are very much alike in flavour so with aesthetic appeal in mind traditional varieties might include 'Long Green Striped', which is striped green and yellow, or 'Table Dainty' which is smaller, sweeter and also has golden-green colouration.

A universally popular **cucumber** selection might include 'Chinese Long Green' or 'Long Green Ridge', which is a heavy cropper.

The variety of **squash and pumpkin** hybrids available to the home gardener is now enormous and they appear in a fascinating range of colours, sizes and shapes. Bred both for their dense, nutty-flavoured flesh, long storage life and decorative appearance, their aesthetic appeal is so valued (particularly in Asian countries) that they may be used as ornaments or incorporated into floral and art displays before being eaten. A highly versatile vegetable, pumpkin may be used grated raw in salads, cooked as soup, purée or soufflé, as a baked vegetable, incorporated into pickles, fried plain in fritters, used in cakes and pies, even prepared as icecream and jam.

Universal favourites among **squash** are the golden 'Sunburst' custard variety which is round and flat with beautifully scalloped edges, and 'Vegetable Spaghetti', a flavoursome hybrid with golden rugby-ball-like fruit which may be stored for many months. A cheerful hybrid to brighten the potager on winter days is the variety 'Hubbard' which is rich gold in colour. A novelty squash now widely available is 'Turk's Turban' which is pinky-orange with green and white stripes and a protruding top that makes it resemble an elaborate turban.

Cucurbits may be easily grown from seed in pots or sown directly into warm moist soils. The fruits, which mature in autumn, may be stored for many months in a cool dark place.

Onions *(Allium cepa)*

Onions, another of the ancient crops, have been said to be the most versatile and used of culinary vegetables. They appear as the traditional flavoursome round globes of varying strengths, non-bulbous upright spring onions and small onions called shallots, which are excellent for pickling. Easy to grow and with a long storage life, modern onion varieties offer harvesting

over an extended period. Unlike other edible crops which deteriorate once they reach their peak, these accommodating vegetables can be harvested when convenient. They serve well as a filler (from sets or transplants), make an attractive edging, and mix happily with carrots, salad greens and tomatoes. Their spear-like leaves form a handsome contrast to vegetables with broad or feathery foliage.

Modern hybrids offer bulbs of deep crimson – 'Brunswick' or 'North Holland Red' are traditional favourites – and for pleasing contrast a block of an old-fashioned pure white variety such as 'Albion' may be planted alongside.

Bronze red lettuce, green cos lettuce and cream and green variegated ornamental kale make colourful and dramatic partners in this beautifully planted vegetable garden.

Onions are ripe for harvesting when the foliage falls over and begins to brown. They should be lightly forked to break the roots, then allowed to dry until the skin is dry and papery. Store in a cool dry place tied in ropes or in open trays.

Spring onions should be sown thickly into open soil and thinned by removing the largest to eat. All onion varieties like a medium to light, well drained rich soil.

Parsnip *(Pastinaca sativa)*

Parsnips are natives of Northern Europe and were a dietary staple before potatoes were introduced. A cold-hardy winter vegetable distantly related to carrots, their foliage is attractively dissected but of a lighter green and their distinctly flavoured roots a creamy-white. The main difference between varieties is the length of the root. Parsnip seed (slow to germinate) may be sown directly into deep fine soil in late spring.

Peas *(Pisum sativum)*

The simple garden pea creates beautiful patterns with its angular silver-green foliage, dainty tendrils, and sweet-smelling flowers of lilac, purple or white, which are followed by swelling pods. There are two main types: smooth or wrinkled seeds for early or later sowing. There are also climbing and dwarf varieties which can be attractively trained and supported on rows or tepees of twiggy branches or over pergolas. The pea is a versatile vegetable, appearing as the tiny 'petit pois', through round, wrinkled, sugar, snap or 'mange tout' peas (harvested young and eaten pods and all), to the substantial 'Marrowfat'. A universally popular mange tout pea is the hybrid 'Carouby de Maussane', with attractive purple flowers and pods which may remain on the plant for weeks without going stringy.

Pea crops enrich the soil with nitrogen, especially if the roots are left in the ground after the crop is harvested. Pea seed may be sown in pots or directly into the ground throughout spring. A good tip is to sow rows in short lengths of gutter pipes and slide them into the bed when the root system has consolidated the seed mix. They require fertile, moisture-retentive but well drained soils. Pea seedlings are unfortunately beloved of mice, slugs and snails, and will need protection in the early stages. I find a ring of coarse sand around each deters the gastropods, and to keep out mice I make small elongated frames of bent chicken wire (blocked at the ends) to enclose the rows of young seedlings.

Potatoes *(Solanum tuberosum)*

Although it is difficult to think of the humble spud as a decorative vegetable, its strong dark green foliage starred with white or purple flowers is pleasing to the eye while it is in season, and the potato crop may be grown behind a row of tall beet or brassicas to conceal the foliage once it starts to die back and look unattractive. Early varieties such as the traditional 'Concorde' may be dug while the foliage is still reasonably fresh and green. Either way, digging potatoes is part of the magic and mystery of gardening!

Potatoes are grown from tubers called seed potatoes. They are gross feeders and need moist soil enriched with compost and manure. When the potatoes are harvested it is beneficial to plant the area with a green manure such as mustard or phacelia.

Radishes *(Raphanus sativus)*

A favourite of the ancient Egyptians, radishes are now grown all over the world, with some Chinese varieties weighing in at around 22 kg (50 lb). The average potagist, however, is more likely to want those tender little red crunchy varieties to enhance summer salads and stir-fries. Summer radishes appreciate a moist, fertile soil, but winter radishes (which can be red, white or black-skinned) require well drained soil. Because they are so quick growing radishes make excellent catch or 'filler in' edibles amongst other crops.

Rhubarb *(Rheum rhabarbarum)*

Rhubarb is a valued resident of the potager for its height, large bold foliage and colourful edible stalks. It counts as one of the garden's most colourful and strongly architectural features, so much so that many gardeners plant it squarely in the flower borders. A perennial that may remain in the same place for many years, rhubarb produces great frills of fat, reddish-tinted leaves. Though attractive, note that they contain high concentrations of oxalic acid and are toxic. As such, they are often used to make

insecticides. Rhubarb dies back in the winter and on the whole prefers a cooler area of the potager and a little shade.

Spinach *(Spinacia oleracea)*

An attractive and prolific crop which may almost be grown year round, spinach bears visually pleasing and highly nutritious rich dark green leaves which vary according to cultivar, from shiny smooth, crinkled, round, to pointed or arrow shaped. A traditional stalwart is the hybrid 'Symphony'.

Spinach germinates and grows very quickly, which makes it an excellent catch crop. It prefers lower temperatures, bolting if the weather turns hot and dry, so is a useful vegetable for growing in the shade of taller vegetables. The plants require rich moisture-retaining soil.

Sweetcorn (maize) *(Zea mays)*

A stand of well grown sweetcorn (or 'sugar corn') is a delight to the eye, the palate, and to the ear as it whispers and rustles in the wind. There can be few vegetables more delicious than the sweet crunchy ears of young corn. Early ripening varieties make cultivation of this crop possible in all but the coldest of areas.

A stand of tall sweetcorn (1.5 m, 4 ft) looks attractive in the middle of a bed, as a border or temporary screen, and lends vertical accents within the potager. Each plant normally only bears two ears which should be harvested when the tassels at the end of the cobs turn black.

Tomatoes *(Lycopersicum lycopersicum)*

Modern tomato hybrids come in an astonishing range of sizes and shapes, and in addition to the traditional gorgeous red colour, vary from hues of green through yellow, to golden orange. Size varies from the giant fruit of the 'Beefsteak' varieties which come on tall plants, through medium size fruit borne by prolific and stalwart varieties such as 'Moneymaker', plum-shaped Italian varieties, to the tiny and deliciously

A mere glimpse of a small cottage emerges from beds planted with vegetables and herbs set in a framework of flowers. The front bed contains broad beans, red and green lettuce, onions, red cabbage and sage. These plantings are repeated in beds to the right, which also contain red Russian kale, beet and chives.

sweet cherry or cocktail tomatoes such as the ever popular 'Sun Cherry' or 'Sweet 100' cultivars borne on compact bushes. For small potagers grow the Japanese mini-bush varieties such as the widely available 'Canary' and 'Red Robin', or 'Tumbler' which looks stunning grown in an urn or hanging basket.

Tomatoes are warm-weather vegetables and need long hours of full sun, moist but well drained fertile soil and lots of watering during dry spells. The seeds need to be started off in pots indoors and not planted out until all risk of frosts have passed. In less temperate areas, tomatoes are deservedly the most popular greenhouse crop.

Turnips (Brassica rapa var. rapa)
Easy to grow, turnips are a hardy vegetable and tolerant enough of cool weather to be planted in late winter. They are useful in the potager for providing blocks and rows of bright green leaves when little else is stirring. The globes of popular cultivars such as 'Purple Top Milan' are white with a rosy flush and look attractive as border plants.

Sow turnip seed thinly into light, loose soil and thin by pulling the largest roots, which may be eaten like radishes.

Berries, vines, pip and stone fruits
Like asparagus, in older potagers soft fruit was generally grown in blocks along the edge of the vegetable garden. Raspberries, gooseberries, blueberries and currants of all colours are suitable even for small potagers but can become invasive if neglected.

A good way to grow small fruit is as an informal hedge along one side of the potager, trained between parallel wires, or on a flat row in fan or lyre shapes.

Gooseberries and currants, bushes with lobed, fuzzy leaves, make attractive free-standing specimens about 1.25–1.5 m (4–5 ft) tall and may be pruned into goblet or arched shapes like small trees. In this form they allow edible plantings underneath, but don't forget to leave enough access to harvest the berries when they are ripe! Today's potager gardener may choose from small fruiting hybrids which come from England, Holland and America.

Left: Young apple trees espaliered over a four-sided ornamental archway will create a delicious edible arbour. The trees are underplanted with companion plantings of nasturtiums and chives.

Opposite: Rhubarb is favoured for both its culinary values and bold architectural foliage. The plant is traditionally placed inside heavy terracotta 'forcer pots' which forces the growth of long fleshy stems. Pots and plants make a striking composition in this large informal potager.

Vines

The traditional vine for the potager is the grape and there is a wealth of varieties with fruit of white, green, amber, rose or purple-black from which to choose. A hardy plant in most soils, given average fertility, grapes will fruit well and are not difficult to grow, but will need the support of wires, frames or ornamental structures. A grapevine is extremely decorative in leaf all season, starting out as fresh green and turning russet-purple in autumn. At the end of the season prune all side shoots to leave two good buds.

Pip and stone fruits

One no longer needs a large garden to be as near self-sufficient for fruit as the climate will allow. Modern trees are a fraction of the size of old-fashioned varieties and, ever mindful of space

for gardens becoming smaller, nurserymen have bred dwarf fruit trees of almost every type – some even bear the same fruit but of two different varieties!

These dwarf cultivars also make excellent container subjects where space is at a premium, or where winters are severe and fruit such as citrus need to be moved to sunny sheltered spots. The larger more traditional varieties will produce just as much fruit in a small potager as they do when they are free-standing if trained into the espalier shapes detailed in Chapter 3. The Quick Reference Guide in Chapter 7 gives further indexed details on fruit and nut growth.

Unusual and delightful ornamental small trees and shrubs (bearing edible fruit) for the potager are the crabapples (*Malus* spp.), the quince (*Cydonia oblonga*) and the japonica or flowering quince (*Chaenomeles* spp.). These

elegant small trees or shrubs bear attractive blossom and foliage and give joyful autumn colour. The shrubs often have an intriguing growth habit and polished bark which presents striking silhouettes in the winter garden. Best of all, quince trees produce wonderful bulbous fruit of red, gold or pale lemon which make excellent conserves and attractive indoor fruit and flower displays. *Malus* cultivars and *Chaenomeles* bear their stunning blossoms on bare branches in late winter when seasonal colour is at a premium.

Please refer to Chapter 7 for a summary of planting design for the potager.

CHAPTER 5

HERBS AND FLOWERS

Herbs

The ancients set great store on the medicinal and fragrant effects of herbs.

Many herbes with their medicine and fragrant sweet smels doe comfort and as it were revive olways ye personne's spirits . . .

Paradisus Terrestris, John Parkinson, 1597

The writings of ancient herbalists such as John Gerard and Nicholas Culpeper form the basis of much of the physical and homeopathic medicine in our modern world. The medieval herb garden was the world's first pharmacy, precious for its collections of medicinal plants, and literally thousands of herbs were ground, mixed, decocted and infused to cure the sick. Powdered yarrow, thyme and woodruff were sniffed like snuff to cure headaches and clear the head. Infusions of basils reduced fevers and coughs were soothed with syrup of honey and hyssop; colds were treated with horehound, sore throats cured with infusions of sage and rosemary. Valerian brought sleep to insomniacs, feverfew relief to migraine sufferers and the seeds of fennel and fenugreek were recommended for nursing mothers. The virtues of herbs were considered almost limitless, especially where they pertained to digestion. Gentian and peppermint in wine were taken for indigestion, rhubarb as a laxative; garlic in milk was a vermifuge for children.

Many herbal remedies which were passed from generation to generation undoubtedly worked, and many modern synthetic compounds in medicines contain the refined forms of the active drugs present in these plants.

Herbs have also been used since earliest

Opposite: Luxuriant edgings of lavender, chives and catmint create colourful borders through the potager herb garden, drawing the visitor towards the ornamental archway at its end.
Above: One can almost smell the pungent perfume of these thymes, intoxicating human visitors and bees alike.

times for dyeing fabric, combating insects both in home and garden, for culinary purposes, and for making pomanders and pot pourri. Tiny tussie mussies of fragrant flowering herbs were given to medieval judges so that they could bury their noses in them to avoid the stench of the prisoners – a trifle hypocritical, since they themselves were not the most fastidious of persons when it came to personal hygiene! People living in draughty medieval dwellings and castles made of stone were not particularly keen on bathing and carried pomanders on their persons to disguise body odours. The mistress of every castle and more affluent home was skilled in the art of herbal medicine. Fresh herbs were strewn on the floors daily so that foot traffic bruised and released their pleasant odours to freshen often ill-lit, ill-ventilated, smoky rooms and to repel flies, lice and fleas.

In times before refrigeration herbs were added to food as preservatives, or to mask the unpleasant tang of spoiling ingredients – to provide a flavour which should have been there but wasn't, or to mask a flavour which was there and shouldn't have been! When meat dishes were less than fresh they were strongly laced with herbs in a disinfecting capacity, in the hope of lessening the ill effects. . . . In addition to use for culinary and medicinal purposes, fragrant herbs such as parsley, mint, thyme and sage were also employed extensively as mouth and breath cleansers, and a bunch of these freshly picked herbs would be placed in the home for the family to use each morning and evening.

Herbs and aromatics are defined as plants used to enhance flavour and are the traditional companion plants of all ornamental vegetable gardens. Their capacity to protect against a variety of insects and diseases, and to stimulate growth, is due to the intensity of the aromatic oils they contain, which are often strongly disinfectant.

Today, herbs are used more for culinary purposes than for medicinal, and when a French chef sends out his assistant to pick a bouquet garni – a bunch of basic herbs – he or she would come back with a basket containing chives and the leaves of mint, chervil, rosemary, parsley, basil, marjoram, coriander, dill, sage, tarragon and thyme, maybe topped off by a colourful bunch of nasturtium flowers for garnishings.

Separate herb gardens

Traditionally, aromatics were planted together in their own beds as well as being used individually within the potager as companion plants. If you are anxious to incorporate as many herbs as possible into your overall planting scheme, a separate bed within the vegetable garden may allow a better display of the elegant formal compositions to which these plants lend themselves so well. They create a delightful tapestry effect with contrasts of foliage colour and texture, highlighted throughout the season with flowers here and there.

When working out a herb garden planting plan it is wise to give attention to the height of each variety at maturity, for aromatics vary tremendously. Fennel or angelica, for example, are tall upright plants, the latter having bold and beautifully dissected foliage of glossy green. Clary sage (*Salvia sclarea*) is another tall and unusual plant bearing deeply veined and textured leaves and fragrant upright flower spires tinted with white, pink and mauve.

It is also a good idea to study which aromatics have powerful and invasive roots, such as mint and oregano, and to be aware of those which self sow readily. Herbs such as these are better contained and controlled in their own separate garden or confined in containers.

Ornamental vegetable gardens often incorporate herbs in a separate bed or as a central focal point. An antique chimney pot planted with tarragon presents a delightful design feature. Herbs include santolina (rear right), chives, red sage, salad burnett, white catmint, pink-flowered thyme, golden lemon thyme, golden oregano, basil and rosemary.

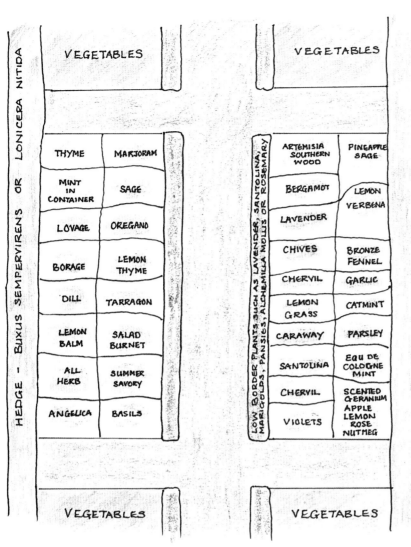

HEDGE – BUXUS SEMPERVIRENS OR LONICERA NITIDA

VEGETABLES   VEGETABLES

THYME	MARJORAM
MINT IN CONTAINER	SAGE
LOVAGE	OREGANO
BORAGE	LEMON THYME
DILL	TARRAGON
LEMON BALM	SALAD BURNET
ALL HERB	SUMMER SAVORY
ANGELICA	BASILS

LOW BORDER PLANTS, SUCH AS LAVENDER, SANTOLINA, MARIGOLDS, PANSIES, ALCHEMILLA MOLLIS OR ROSEMARY

ARTEMISIA SOUTHERN WOOD	PINEAPPLE SAGE
BERGAMOT	LEMON VERBENA
LAVENDER	
CHIVES	BRONZE FENNEL
CHERVIL	GARLIC
LEMON GRASS	CATMINT
CARAWAY	PARSLEY
SANTOLINA	EAU DE COLOGNE MINT
CHERVIL	SCENTED GERANIUM
VIOLETS	APPLE LEMON ROSE NUTMEG

VEGETABLES   VEGETABLES

The design for the central herb beds presented here may be adapted from either square or rectangular shapes. The beds form a pair of both culinary and fragrant borders alongside a pathway. Each half may be used separately within other areas (such as the four corners or two diagonally opposite corners) of the potager. Care must be taken to place the taller herbs, such as borage, common fennel, geranium and pineapple sage, at the back of the beds near the hedge. This design is well suited to perennial herbs which may be interplanted with annual aromatics according to the season.

Planning herb beds within the potager
Two simple designs for a herb garden

A herb garden is often used to create the centrepiece of the potager. The traditional circular bed shown here is based on the simple wheel, or rays of the sun, designs which were popular in medieval times. The design works equally well laid out in bricks or as an open bed bordered by dwarf hedges of box, lonicera or lavenders. A variation which is visually pleasing is to encircle the central ring with hedging synonymous to the outer. This design is best planted with herbs of low to medium height. The plantings are suggestions only, and may be varied to suit individual climate and preference.

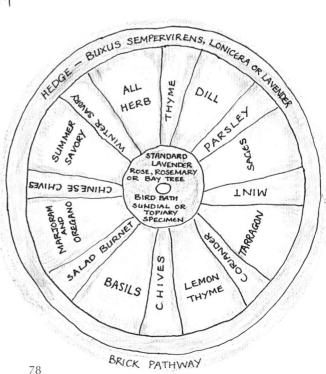

HEDGE – BUXUS SEMPERVIRENS, LONICERA OR LAVENDER

ALL HERB · THYME · DILL · PARSLEY · SAGES · MINT · TARRAGON · CORIANDER · LEMON THYME · CHIVES · BASILS · SALAD BURNET · MARJORAM AND OREGANO · CHINESE CHIVES · WINTER SAVORY · SUMMER SAVORY

STANDARD LAVENDER ROSE, ROSEMARY OR BAY TREE
BIRD BATH SUNDIAL OR TOPIARY SPECIMEN

BRICK PATHWAY

Both designs opposite offer an aesthetically pleasing and productive display, and may be adapted in size to suit one's own particular site and the plantings of herbs varied to suit personal culinary preferences.

Most herbs require warm sheltered positions, so beds must be sited in full sun. It is also for this reason that gardens containing medicinal and culinary plants traditionally have always been walled or bordered by dwarf hedges. Herbs give the best of their aromatic oils in the micro-climate created by an enclosed area of full sunshine. Step into such a herb garden and instantly become as drowsy and intoxicated as the bees!

It is a fallacy that most herbs will thrive in poor dry soil, but true that many require light, well-drained soils not enriched by fertilisers. Herbs need to be harvested frequently to promote constant new growth, and for this reason thought should be given to providing those you use most with readily accessible positions.

Favourite edible herbs

The list of herbs that follow is by no means exhaustive but includes those used most extensively in home cuisine. Edible herbs treasured as insect repellent or attractant companion plants are discussed in Chapter 8.

Basil (*Ocimum basilicum*) is considered an indispensable decorative herb throughout the world, coming in diverse foliage colours, sizes and flavours. The most popular introduction in recent years has been the stunning purple-black hybrid 'Purple Ruffles'. For striking plant association combine its garnet glory with the lime-green foliage of feverfew (*Chrysanthemum parthenium* 'Aureum'). 'Dark Opal' is another purple-black leaved basil. Basil 'Green Ruffles' is similar in leaf form and flavour to 'Purple Ruffles'. Height to 60 cm (2 ft). Basils require warm sunny positions, moist but well drained soils. Not cold hardy, so sow as annuals in colder areas. Said to keep mildew off cucurbits.

Other types of basil include **anise basil**: its pretty mulberry-tinted leaves, with rich aroma of anise, give subtle flavour to salads and sauces. Upright bushy plant. Lavender flowers make edible garnishes. **Bush basil** (*O. minimum*) is a compact dwarf basil with small fine leaves, suitable for planting in pots. It will crop most of the year indoors and in warm areas. Basil 'Fino Verde' is a most popular pungent bush basil used extensively in Italian cuisine. **Cinnamon basil** (*O. basilicum* spp.) from Mexico has a distinctive cinnamon taste and odour. **Genovese basil** is a broad-leafed sweet Italian basil, suitable for drying. Basil is a prodigious family and it is possible to acquire a tastebud-tantalising collection.

Bay (*Laurus nobilis*) was a shrub revered by ancient Romans for diverse decorative and culinary purposes, and for crowning poets and scholars! The plant is an attractive container subject and may be trained to make impressive standards; it will grow to a small tree if left unclipped. Rich green glossy leaves impart excellent flavour to casseroles, soups and stews. Hardy to most soils, the bay tolerates dry conditions but is very slow growing.

Borage (*Borago officinalis*) offers luxuriant tiered foliage of greyish-green with a cucumber-like flavour which may be used young in salads or cooked like spinach. The herb's exquisite deep blue, black-eyed flowers may be popped into ice-cube trays to decorate and cool summer drinks, or used as garnishes. Self sows readily; hardy; full sun. Height to 1 m (3 ft). Keep trimmed for compact growth.

Chamomile (*Matricaria recutita* syn. *chamomilla*) (German). This upright plant 30–50 cm (12–20 in) high has dainty thread-like foliage and small daisy-like flowers from which popular herbal tea is made. **Creeping (Roman) chamomile** (*Chamaemelum nobile*) is an evergreen perennial used as a groundcover, spreading readily, and bearing small daisy-like flowers and filigree foliage. Self sows. Hardy. Non-flowering variety *C. n.* 'Treneague' makes a fragrant lawn or surface for a bench or seat.

Chervil (*Anthriscus cerefolium*), brought to England and Europe by the Romans, is a low-growing (30 cm, 1 ft), annual umbellifer containing large amounts of Vitamin C. It has very fine delicate foliage and bears heads of small dainty white flowers. Self sows once established, making an attractive filler between other vegetables.

Chervil root (*Chaerophyllum bulbosum*) This hardy plant is highly sought after by French chefs for its delicately flavoured bulbous stems and roots. The variety 'Brussels Winter' is a cool-weather variety, compact in growth and slow bolting. Both varieties require semi-shade and moist soil to prevent bolting. Grows to 1.5 m (5 ft).

Chives (*Allium schoenoprasum*) Decorative and culinary, chives make a delightful edger in the potager and will clump up quickly if regularly divided. Lavender pompom heads adored by the bees lend the foil of colour against the greens of the vegetables. Height to 30 cm (1 ft). Hardy. **Chinese chives** (*A. tuberosum*) have attractive white starry flowers and their spears are slightly flattened. This herb is rich in iron and sulphur, a mild antibiotic and helps digestion of fatty foods. In his fifteenth-century *Compleat English Herballe* the ancient herbalist John Gerard defined chives thus: 'Chives hath both the smell and taste of onion and leeke, as it were participating in both.'

Coriander (*Coriandrum sativum*), also called cilantro or Chinese parsley, is an annual umbellifer extensively used in Thai, Chinese, Mexican, African, French and American cuisine, though it is a flavour not favoured by other European peoples. This ancient herb is mentioned in the Old Testament. An attractive plant with delicate, finely dissected foliage and clouds of small white flowers, its mature seeds are ground and used extensively in many forms of cuisine. Requires a sunny situation and moderately good soil. Grows to 45 cm (18 in).

Dill (*Anethum graveolens*) Native of the Mediterranean and Southern Russia, this is an attractive annual herb bearing fine filmy foliage and umbels of yellow flowerheads with a strong aromatic scent. All parts are edible and rich in vitamins. Self sows. Height 90 cm (33 in). A dwarf variety suitable for containers and tiny-space potagers is **fernleaf dill,** which grows to 45 cm (18 in) and is slow to bolt. Needs a dry sunny position sheltered from winds.

Fennel (*Foeniculum vulgare*) With a rich aniseed flavour, fennel has seeds which are crushed and used in both sweet and savoury dishes. Attractive filmy bronze foliage is used with salads, fish and meat, and as garnishes. Fennel self sows freely and can become invasive and hard to dig up – remove seedheads! Perennial to 180 cm (6 ft).

Feverfew (*Chrysanthemum parthenium*) Feverfew is from 'febrifuge', a medieval term meaning an agent to drive away fevers. The common variety has light green foliage and small white daisy flowers with golden centres, and *C. parthenium* 'Aureum' is popular for its attractive light lime-green foliage. Feverfew has a strong and bitter taste. It has been used for many centuries in the treatment of migraine headaches. Hardy in poor soils. Self sows. Height to 50 cm (20 in).

Garlic (*Allium sativum*) This herb has been in cultivation since ancient times and is considered one of the most valuable herbs known to man. International medical scientists and pharmaceutical companies today pour millions of dollars into research, believing garlic can reduce

Creating a pleasing tapestry, informal plantings of massed herbs release the fragrance of their essential oils to the sun. Red sage, *Salvia officinalis* var. *purpurea*, which has plum-coloured leaves with a soft purple bloom and dark blue flowers, dominates the front border. To the left, the massed pink flowers of common thyme create a pleasing underplanting for the purple sage.

cholesterol levels, inhibit blood clots, ease asthma, prevent strokes and treat tumours. Grown as an annual by splitting the bulbs into individual cloves and planting each year, garlic requires full sun and fertile well drained soil. Height 30 cm (1 ft). See also Chapter 4.

Horseradish (*Armoracia rusticana*), a hardy perennial to 40 cm (16 in), creates a clump of exotic-looking leaves. Roots are harvested once a year but can never be entirely removed. The flavour of the grated root is so strong that is was called 'monk's mustard' in ancient times. Grown from crown cuttings taken from top 5 cm (2 in) of the mature root. Requires moist rich soil.

Hyssop (*Hyssopus officinalis*) This small evergreen bush (to 30 cm, 1 ft) deserves more recognition, having stunning bright blue, pink or white scented spiked flowers, which attract the bees, and small narrow green leaves. Used in cooking with beans, in stuffings, soups, sauces

and egg dishes and for herb teas. Requires sunny position and fertile well drained soil.

Lemon balm (*Melissa officinalis*) has prettily indented foliage and small white flowers. Height to 60 cm (2 ft). Requires light trimming to keep plant compact. Can be invasive. Foliage makes good tea. Young leaves are a pleasant and unusual addition to salads. Attractive variegated and golden-leaved varieties are widely available. Hardy. Best confined in a container to restrict root growth.

Lovage (*Levisticum officinale*) A handsome hardy perennial whose hollow stems can be used like celery. Leaves have a spicy peppery taste and are used in soups, stews and casseroles. Seeds give spicy flavour to cakes, biscuits and bread. Easily grown from seed or from root pieces, lovage requires rich moist soil that allows easy root penetration. Cold hardy. Grows to 2 m (7 ft).

One can almost smell the sweet and spicy odours which the sunshine has released from the essential oils of the plants in this luxuriant herb garden. The tapestry includes purple-red sage, variegated golden sage, rosemary, angelica, scented geraniums, catmint and bronze fennel.

Marjoram (*Origanum majorana*) and **oregano** (*O. vulgare*) are closely related. *O. majorana*, also known as sweet marjoram, is a half-hardy perennial making a compact bush 40 cm (16 in) high, of greyish round aromatic and flavoursome leaves. Used to flavour fish, cheese, tomato and meat dishes, this variety's leaves also dry well. Oregano has a sharper taste, heart-shaped opposite leaves and delicate pink flowers. It grows to 60 cm (2 ft) and makes a good groundcover in dry soils, though it can be invasive. **Pot marjoram** (*O. onites*) is a perennial herb to 60 cm (2 ft). It is the easiest marjoram to grow, has a delicate flavour, and small pale pink or white flowers highly attractive to bees. Marjorams require a rich soil and warm position in full sun.

Mint (*Mentha viridis rotundifolia*) is the 'roast lamb' mint and probably the most popular variety of this large species, of which the Roman naturalist Pliny wrote 'it do stir up men's minds to the most greedy desire of meat'. Mints are best planted in pots to confine their invasive root systems. Many varieties of this herb are available. Two of the most decorative are the **cream-green variegated apple mint** (delicious with pork) and the fragrant **eau-de-cologne mint**, which has dark purplish-green foliage. A handful of bruised leaves in the tired gardener's bath does wonders for aching bones! Hardy. Grows to 50 cm (20 in).

Parsley (*Petroselinum crispum*) is a biennial umbellifer rich in iron and vitamins. It is easily grown, but seed takes a notoriously long time to germinate and old garden folklore says it goes to the devil and back first! Soaking seeds for 48 hours before planting is recommended. Many decorative varieties of this highly nutritious and popular herb are available worldwide, including **plain-leaf parsley** (*Petroselinum hortense*), which, unlike common curly-leaf parsley, has plain flat leaves that dry well and have a strong but smoother flavour. **Hamburg parsley** (*Petroselinum crispum* var. *tuberosum*), referred to as 'parsnip-rooted parsley', has roots resembling small parsnips and may be eaten as a winter vegetable. **Parsley exotic-curled/Triple curled** offers dark green leaves on strong compact plants, especially attractive for garnishes. Cold hardy, producing new growth in low temperatures. **Parsley 'Gigantic Italian'** (*Petroselinum crispum* var. *neapolitan*) has big, deep green, shiny leaves with an exceptionally sweet and fuller flavour than standard varieties, and grows to 80 cm (2 ft 8 in). Parsley leaves are excellent in all cooked dishes and delicious in salads. The stalks may be crunched like celery.

Purple perilla (*Perilla frutescens* var. *crispa*), known as *shisho* in Japan and 'summer coleus' in the USA, is an exciting addition to the potager. A highly attractive foliage plant, used originally in Victorian bedding-out schemes, it is now a popular culinary herb in oriental countries, especially Japan. Both leaves and seeds emit a pleasant spicy cinnamon odour caused by an organic compound within the plant called perilla aldehyde, an oil 2000 times sweeter than sugar. Wrinkled dark burgundy foliage, heavily veined with crimson-pink, is sharply indented along the edges and reminiscent of that of the common ornamental coleus. Grows to 50 cm (20 in). There is also a **green-leafed perilla** which has a delicious peppery flavour. Easy to grow, but seed needs light and chilling at 5°C in moist sand to effect germination. Pinching out flower spikes keeps the plant compact and encourages colourful fresh new foliage.

Rosemary (*Rosmarinus officinalis*) Growing to 120 cm (3 ft 4 in), this hardy shrubby perennial with sky-blue flowers and narrow grey-green aromatic foliage is loved by bees. The prostrate variety looks superb trailing from the top of walls or large raised containers. French chefs decree that roast lamb without rosemary is a culinary sin! Thrives in impoverished soils but requires good drainage.

Sage (*Salvia officinalis*), a hardy perennial growing to 60 cm (2 ft), is available in three ornamental culinary varieties, all bearing attractive purple-blue flowers beloved of beneficial insects. One variety has purplish-red leaves, another yellow-flecked, and a third has beautifully variegated foliage of cream, pink and green. The **yellow-leafed sage** (*Salvia officinalis* 'Icterina') is hardy in most situations. Sages occasionally die back unexpectedly, but cuttings from the parent plant root easily so the gap is filled fairly quickly. The sages require well drained soil and full sun.

Tarragon (*Artemisia dracunculus*) Described as 'the king of herbs', tarragon is a culinary must in any potager. In flavour, **Russian tarragon** is said to be inferior to the **French** variety (*A. d.* var. *sativa*) but has the advantage of being able to be propagated from seed. The latter may be propagated from a mature plant in autumn. This herb has finely dissected long narrow leaves

Catmint underplants the circular border of double white feverfew daisies enclosing the vegetable beds. Planted with red and green lettuces, beetroot, brassicas, globe artichokes and other vegetables, the beds are bordered with a perfumed framework of old roses, foxgloves and mignonette.

which have no odour until cut. The Russian variety has panicles of tiny yellow-green flowers and needs regular light trimming to keep it compact. The herb is used extensively in fish, chicken and meat dishes, also stuffings, salads, vinegar and mayonnaise. Requires sunny sheltered position and well drained light soil, where it will grow to 60 cm (2 ft).

Thyme (*Thymus vulgaris*) is a perennial growing between 8 and 30 cm (3 in–1 ft), but for the potager **bush thyme** is usually less than 30 cm (1 ft). Bearing pink or white flowers on fine, silvery foliage, it requires clipping to keep a compact shape and promote new growth. **Creeping thyme** (*Thymus serpyllum*) 1–5 cm (1–2 in) prefers acid, stony soil and carpets flat surfaces or will fall attractively over low walls. *Thymus pulegiodes* 'Aureus' has foliage variegated green and gold, and is hardy in poor soils. Creeping thymes are popular for planting between pavers so that their rich pungent oils are released by foot traffic; be aware that bees

This exciting colour-coded potager offers an electrifying combination of vegetables, herbs and flowers. Petunias, New Guinea impatiens, parsley, celosia and the tall salvia 'Bonfire' make an underplanting of vibrant reds and pinks for a colourful clump of purple-red rainbow beet occupying the centre bed. To the left, crimson canna lilies and the burgundy foliage and red flowers of a perennial dahlia provide strong contrast with dark green and grey speckled zucchini foliage. To the right, dwarf beans and tomatoes are bordered with salmon-pink achillea flowers, red salvia and dahlias.

are also particularly fond of this herb when it is in flower so resist the temptation to walk barefoot even if it is midsummer! Although hardy, all thymes need full sun and good drainage.

Flowers in the potager

The idea of decorative vegetable gardening conjures up a vision of bright flowers combined with vegetables. Such intermingling was common in the cloistered gardens of medieval castles and monasteries, and from this evolved the English cottage garden. In Victorian and Edwardian days various flowers were used as seasonal indicators. Cucurbits were sown when mock orange (*Philadelphus*) bloomed, tomatoes when hawthorn blossomed, and corn when the apple blossom fell.

As companion plants, herbs and flowers bring many practical benefits as well as beauty to the potager, but care needs to be taken with the quantity that are grown and whether they are invasive or self-sowing – the object is not to have them overpowering or in direct competition with the veges. Another prime reason for growing certain flowers with the vegetables is, of course, because one intends to eat them. There are flowers to add to salads, including borage, calendula, lavender, rosemary, nasturtiums, roses and daylilies. We also grow flowers to make garnishes, aromatic oils, teas, vinegars and waters for cooking or salad dressings.

Further benefits derived from growing flowers in the potager are attributed to the fact that, like herbs, the perfumes of the essential oils of certain flowers, when released by the sun, stimulate the growth of near-by vegetables – pot marigolds (*Calendula*) next to tomatoes, for example, or they may enrich the soil by adding to it nitrogen or mineral properties. A line of lupins sown among thirsty salad stuffs is recommended for providing light shade and for fixing extra nitrogen in the soil. Many flowers are used for companion planting, protecting neighbouring plants from pests and diseases (see Chapter 8).

Some edible flowers are perennials and need to be situated where their roots will not be disturbed. Low-growing plants can often share space with fruit trees or be used as edgings for

Borage Height 1 m (3 ft). Hardy to most soils. Prefers full sun. Keep tips pinched to maintain compact plant. Use tender new cucumber-flavoured leaves in salads, or cook as for spinach. Drop the tiny brilliant blue flowers into ice-cube trays for summer drinks, and use as dainty garnishes. Self sows freely.

Calendula (pot marigold) Height 30–60 cm (1–2 ft). Hardy. Has edible many-petalled flowers of cream, yellow or orange which can be used as a substitute for saffron in rice, for stuffings, herb butters, or in garnishes and cooked dishes.

Marigolds (dwarf) To 28 cm (11 in). Hardy, but prefers well drained soils. These tagetes flowers are similar to those of French marigolds (which are not edible), but more delicate, less brassy and often have lovely velvety textures. They are used extensively in the potager as insect repellents and attractants and for their warm colours which contrast beautifully with the darker green of vegetable leaves. The widely available varieties *Tagetes tenuifolia* 'Lemon Gem' and 'Tangerine Gem' are edible and have a citrus-like odour and flavour which make a pleasing addition to salads and desserts.

Nasturtiums Height 30 cm (1 ft). Dwarf or climbing varieties are all useful, and the old hybrid 'Alaska' has foliage marbled cream and green. Nasturtiums have attractive rounded and veined foliage, and gay red, orange and yellow spurred trumpet flowers freely produced over a long period. They will bolt and form abundant foliage rather than flowers if given rich damp soils, so are best sown under edible plants which do not require copious watering. Tender new leaves give salads a pleasant peppery flavour, the seedheads, picked before they are too old, can be pickled like capers, and the flowers used as dramatic garnishes in salads and cold dishes. Nasturtiums look most attractive scrambling up climbing beans and as an underplanting to tomatoes.

beds of perennial vegetables such as artichokes, rhubarb or asparagus.

Four valuable flowering annuals

Four flowering plants which are immensely valuable in the potager include *Calendula officinalis* (pot marigold), *Tagetes tenuifolia* (note: *not* all varieties of marigolds are edible), borage (*Borago officinalis*), and nasturtium (*Tropaeolum majus*). In addition to being aesthetically pleasing and edible, they repel undesirable insects and attract beneficial ones, stimulate the growth of other plants with their pungent perfumes and, in the case of calendula and tagetes, discourage nematodes in the soil.

Decorative aromatics with showy flowers

A particularly important category of decorative aromatics are those which have the added bonus of showy flowers. These are treasured in the ornamental garden because on the whole the flowers of herbs are generally inconspicuous. Most are grown for the medicinal and nutritional values contained in their oily aromatic foliage.

A much loved and versatile family is the **catmint** group (*Nepeta* spp.), from the tall, white-flowered *Nepeta cataria*, to the prostrate, purplish-blue *Nepeta* x *faassenii* and the cultivar 'Six Hills Giant', which makes luxuriant clumps up to 1 m (3 ft) high and wide. The catmints will flower again if regularly trimmed. All are adored by beneficial insects – and cats!

The yellow flowers of **tansy** (*Tanacetum vulgare*) make an attractive colour combination with blue-flowered catmint. It looks rather like yellow achillea with somewhat smaller clumps (60 cm, 2 ft) and dries well for floral decoration. It is the most vigorous of self sowers, but its leaves make an efficient organic insecticide.

Bergamot, also called perennial horsemint or bee balm (*Monarda didyma*), grows to 60–80 cm (24–33 in) high and comes with striking shaggy flowers of vibrant deep reds, purple or blue. It is a perennial that appreciates moister soils.

Roses for vertical interest

Apart from our general enslavement by the rose, repeated plantings of **standard or patio roses** in the potager are valued for giving both symmetry and vertical interest in formal designs. While it may be considered a bit over the top in the home potager, standard roses are used in a most dramatic manner at Château Villandry in France. Each of the four sections of the huge potager has 36 standard roses, many of them of a rich dark red, above the multicoloured squares of vegetables.

The *rugosa* species is also an excellent addition to the potager, having heavily textured dark green foliage and single to semi-double exquisitely perfumed petals of red, white or pink.

Disease-resistant, they do not require spraying and need little pruning. The rugosa have highly ornamental heps which are rich in Vitamin C, etc. They make excellent hedges or screens. Height to 1.5 m (5 ft). Favourite varieties include 'Blanc Double de Coubert' (fragile, tissue-like white petals bossed with gold stamens),

The raised bed of this informal and appealing potager is planted with nasturtiums (right), double feverfew and borage (left). At the centre, the bed is block planted with red and green lettuces. A clump of bold rainbow beet and purple-red sage make the perfect companions for the plum-wine roses 'Chianti' and 'Cardinal Hume'. Pink roses provide a further colour foil to the rich greens of the vegetables and ensure that perfume pervades the potager and herb garden in the time-honoured tradition.

'Frau Dagmar Hastrup' (silver-pink), and 'Roseraie de l'Hay' (intoxicating perfume, luscious deep crimson-red petals).

The rose which is a must in the potager if space allows is the ancient *Rosa gallica officinalis* – 'the apothecary's rose'. From earliest times the clear crimson-pink richly fragrant petals of this unique rose have been used for medicinal and culinary purposes and for toiletries. Growing to approximately 1 m (3 ft), the bush makes an attractive centrepiece.

Tall flowers for the potager

Tall flowers are valued in the potager for their aesthetic appeal, their ability to provide screens, dividers and vertical accents, and in some cases, of course, for their edible properties.

Sunflowers The French artist Claude Monet planted whole walls of sunflowers in his garden for the sheer joy of painting them. Famous French gardener Colette Lafon (1873–1954) described sunflowers as having 'hearts like black enamel', and grew them draped with sky-blue morning glories – a strikingly unusual plant association, but if one has a mind to try this, it would be prudent to confine any species of convolvulus in containers, or to check carefully that the seeds are of a cultivated, non-invasive hybrid.

Love-lies-bleeding (*Amaranthus* spp.) I have never fathomed why this attractive plant genus should be saddled with such a gruesome common name. Until recently regarded purely as a flowering plant, many amaranthus species are now cultivated for use in underdeveloped countries as a much-valued food source, the leaves used as spinach, and the seeds as a high-protein grain crop.

Amaranthus have always been grown in the flower garden for their visually appealing and brilliantly coloured flower tassels and spires. Now that their food potential is realised, they have become both an edible and ornamental asset to the potager.

Amaranths are usually tall growing annuals and about 15 varieties are readily available from seed catalogues worldwide. *Amaranthus retroflexus* (**redroot**), with attractive red stems, grows to about 30 cm (1 ft) and is usually raised as a vegetable. The ornamental *Amaranthus caudatus* (**love-lies-bleeding**) and **prince's feather** (*A. hypochondriacus* syn. *A. hybridus* var. *erythrostachys*) both give grain as well as dark crimson to reddish-brown flowers and tender young leaves and grow about 1–1.2 m (3–3½ ft) tall. The variety most valued for grain production is *A. cruentus*.

The leaf varieties are from 30 cm–1 m (1–3 ft) tall and include *A. gangetus*, known in the Caribbean as **calabou**. Although the leaves of grain amaranths are edible, those of leaf amaranths are particularly nutritious. All have leaf

Left: Parsley and capsicum underplant vibrant orange-red zinnias and tagetes marigolds at left. To the right, an edging of calendula borders a row of dark purple basil, capsicum and beet. A stand of sunflowers provides vertical accent.

Opposite: Treasured from earliest times for its beauty and perfume, luxuriant borders of royal purple old English lavender billow over the pathway through this edible garden.

and inflorescence colours which range from green through gold to burgundy.

In the potager a bank or bed of port-wine-coloured amaranths is an impressive sight with their impossibly long tassels or spires of millions of tiny flowers offering dramatic contrast of colour, form and foliage amongst the more prosaic vegetable varieties. An added bonus is that birds love their seeds – distracting them from one's tender new lettuce seedlings!

Amaranths do best in soil with high organic content and will give their all in a slightly acid or lime-free position since they have a high nitrogen absorption rate. They respond to a booster dressing, are drought tolerant but will be cut down by the first hard frost.

Hollyhocks (*Althea rosea*) Another tall-growing flower (to 1.5 m, 5 ft) favoured in English and European potagers is the old-fashioned hollyhock – not the frilly double modern hybrids but the old singles. I am particularly fond of the variety *Althea rosea* 'Nigra' which has flowers so dark as to be almost black. The tiered height of this plant and the contrast of its dramatic dark blooms against large light-green foliage make it a delightful garden resident.

Globe artichokes (*Cynara scolymus*) and **cardoons** (*C. cardunculus*) Though strictly more vegetable than flowers, the globe artichoke and cardoons (height up to 2 m, 7 ft), provide powerful architectural interest in the potager. They bear silver foliage and dramatic thistle-like buds

which, if left to bloom, become silken-tufted purple flowers. Their dried heads are keenly sought after for floral decoration. Both species require rich soil and frequent watering. Cardoons are grown for their thick white edible stems, unlike the artichoke, which is cultivated for its delicious globe head. The **Jerusalem artichoke** (*Helianthus tuberosus*), a tall handsome plant grown for its edible tubers rather than its head, bears large golden-yellow sunflower-type blooms.

Some vegetables themselves flower beautifully. The **squash family** has warm yellow chalices among luxuriant green foliage, and both these and zucchini flowers are served with savoury stuffings in European cuisine or used in salads and as garnishes. The fruit of both species, smooth or rough, green or yellow, dark or speckled, are all attractive in their own right.

Onions, leeks and **chives** also offer attractive blooms, although they are not usually allowed to flower – in the interests of harvesting! The flowers of **climbing beans** are also highly ornamental. If you have planted more of a vegetable crop than your family requires, allow some to run to seed. You will be pleasantly surprised at the enormous variety and beauty of vegetable flowers. **Chicory**, for example, sports enchanting daisy flowers of clearest blue.

For other herbs and flowers suitable for potager cultivation, please see the Quick Reference Guide in Chapter 7.

CHAPTER 6

NO-SOIL AND TINY-SPACE GARDEN

As living space diminishes in our modern world, houses become smaller and many people live in high-rise buildings or in small urban dwellings. If your space for a potager is in an inner-city courtyard, an urban 'pocket handkerchief', or on a 'no-soil' veranda, rooftop or patio site – read on! In these locations, the immense versatility offered by container gardening affords the small-space potagist the pleasure of having homegrown vegetables, herbs, flowers and even dwarf fruit trees.

Opposite: This productive and innovative small potager, where the traditional and modern stand side by side, illustrates bold design concepts in a restricted space.
Above: Container plants can add colour and excitement to the smallest corner. Red salvia and red and white geraniums provide a colourful framework for this highly ornamental capsicum, *C. 'Long Sweet Yellow'*.

Creating edible gardens in containers

Almost all vegetables can be grown in containers and grow-bags (see page 95). Most gardeners traditionally grow herbs in pots but even a crop such as potatoes can be grown in a 10 litre (2 gallon) plastic bucket, cut-down dustbin or an old barrel. Aware of ever diminishing garden space, seedsmen are concentrating on hybridising vegetable varieties which are smaller in growth habit, but big on yield. There is presently an exciting range of gourmet baby vegetables and dwarf varieties at our disposal.

Carrots, radishes, beetroots, dwarf beans, aubergines/eggplants, courgettes/zucchini, cucurbits, capsicums, chilli peppers, onions and brassicas comprise a few of these smaller edibles and the list that follows is not exhaustive.

Capsicums, chillies and aubergines grow on compact bushes which rarely exceed 1 m (3 ft), thus making highly decorative and prolific container or small-space subjects. Tomatoes, which come in an amazing variety of sizes, are especially successful in tubs, pots or grow-bags. Among the root vegetables, traditional stalwarts such as carrots, beetroot, radish, parsnips and kohlrabi, etc., now come in globe-rooted forms which may be sown in shallower troughs and thinned out in the normal way.

Most cucurbits require a container about 30 cm (1 ft) in diameter and 30 cm (1 ft) deep. They will require a trellis or some support to climb up. A grouping of 3–4 dwarf bean bushes or six climbing varieties at the foot of a tepee in a large container 30 x 25 cm (12 x 9 in), or in a small bed, will crop prolifically if picked regularly. (See wooden tepee/planter box design, Chapter 2.) The cultivation of 'vertical veg' leaves precious ground space free for the underplanting of other crops, or for the grouping of smaller pots containing herbs and companion plants beneath.

Larger varieties of the taller capsicums, tomatoes, cauliflowers, broccolis, marrows, pumpkins and other cucurbits need large pots 35–60 cm (13–24 in) in diameter and 25–40 cm (9–16 in) deep. Old half barrels, built-in planter boxes or fibreglass water tanks (remember to insert drainage holes!) hold small groupings of larger vegetables such as cauliflowers and single plants of sprouting broccoli which, with regular picking, will crop over a long period. A universally popular broccoli for growing in small spaces is 'Raab', and a grouping of one each of an early, middle and late season variety will give

Top left: Three deep containers placed end to end create a bed planted with salad stuffs, beet and herbs.
Middle left: Courgettes/zucchini, tomatoes and zinnias grow happily in an old bath, a hanging basket supports a dwarf tomato, and other containers hold a variety of herbs and vegetables.
Left: These cheerful containers are planted with (right to left) red chillies, tall lemon grass, red zinnias, variegated apple mint, red zinnias, tansy, chives, lettuce, parsley, purple sage, rosemary, nasturtiums, salsify and blue salvias – the ultimate in 'no soil' potagers.

almost year round crops even in the container garden. For the small-space or container potager standard cauliflowers are a large vegetable which takes a long time to mature, but two universally popular dwarf varieties are 'Alpha' and 'Idol', which may be grown in medium-sized containers or in small beds just 15 cm (6 in) apart. They should be harvested when the heads are tennis-ball size.

Pots or troughs about 15 cm (6 in) in diameter and 15–20 cm (6–9 in) deep are suitable for smaller vegetables and herbs. Most bought troughs are approximately 20 cm (7 in) wide and vary in length from 30 cm (1 ft) to 90 cm (3 ft). These may be used for more shallow-rooting vegetables such as self-blanching celery, salad stuffs, oriental brassicas, beetroot, kales, silverbeet and spinach. Chinese greens are compact in growth habit and mature quickly, which makes them excellent container subjects.

Beet and spinach plants are ideal for container and small-space cultivation since they are shallow rooted and have vertical growth habits. For big healthy plants which may be cropped on the 'pick and come again' basis, grow one to a pot, approximately 30 x 25 cm (12 x 9 in) or space 30 cm (1 ft) apart in nitrogenous rich soil. They require regular watering in dry weather to prevent bolting.

Even with a no-soil or pocket-handkerchief potager, continuous crops can be had by successive sowing of vegetable seeds in smaller pots to replace plants which have been harvested. It is therefore important to budget for space for a sunny, sheltered 'nursery corner' where seedlings can be tended easily and frequently. With replacement seedlings, the growing season can be as extended and the crop yield as fruitful as that from a medium-sized garden potager.

Hints for small-space gardening success

To gain maximum output and continuous production from the space you have available, the following ideas will help you get larger and better crops and sustained yield.

Well fed and watered climbing beans grow happily in a terracotta pot, providing both vertical accent and a focal point.

1. Position your potager where it will receive the maximum amount of sunshine.
2. Grow as many vegetables as you can vertically to maximise space.
3. Choose varieties that suit your own soil and region.
4. If your soil is heavy or poorly drained use timber or bricks to raise your beds.
5. Stagger your sowing and planting for a continuous supply of crops.
6. Grow vegetable varieties which have been bred for small spaces or container growth.
7. Increase soil fertility with homemade or commercially prepared manure and compost.
8. Keep pests and diseases at bay with a strict hygiene routine.
9. Grow beans and peas in a tepee style for all-round exposure to light.
10. Ask your nurseryman to recommend dwarf varieties which are also heavy croppers.
11. Use cloches and cold frames both early and late in the season to extend growing periods.
12. Above all, remember that containerised crops need maximum sunshine, regular watering and feeding to maximise yield and harvesting.

Making a mini-cloche and a row cloche

To protect replacement seedlings in pots early in the season, make a mini-cloche by bending a loop in a length of number 8 wire about the same diameter as the pot's top, making sure you have left a wire leg long enough to push into the soil, compost or potting mix. Draw a plastic bag over the loop of wire and tie to the pot with string or large rubber band.

To make a simple cloche for a row of vegetables, bend lengths of number 8 wire into hoops to the desired depth, that is, with enough head space to allow the plants to develop. Push the wires into the soil at regular intervals and then thread an elongated sheet of clear polythene over and under the hoops to prevent the wind lifting it off. Tie ends loosely. Simple and inexpensive cloches such as this protect tender seedlings against slugs and snails as well as the vagaries of the elements.

Building a basic cold frame

The number of pieces of planking you will require obviously depends upon the desired size and height of your frame. The rear wall should be built higher than the front to accommodate taller seedlings. The side struts will need to be angled to meet the lower front wall. The cover may be constructed of a length of heavy-duty clear polythene attached at either end to a light batten. An even more basic design would be a square or rectangle of four planks of wood with an old window or piece of glass hinged onto or resting on top.

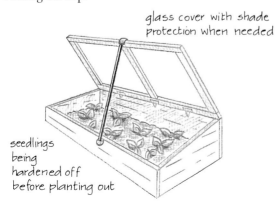

glass cover with shade protection when needed

seedlings being hardened off before planting out

Trolley for upwardly mobile plants

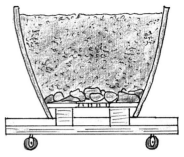

One of the great advantages of container gardening is that plants can be moved easily, but a soil-filled container can be heavy. If you have a no-soil garden situation it is worth considering mounting all but the smallest containers on a simple trolley made of a flat piece of wood fitted with four furniture castors and a rope handle, which can help to avoid back injury. Tilt one side of the container, push the trolley under, then ease on the other side of the pot. Garden centres offer a range of custom-made devices on wheels for this purpose. The mobility of a container garden means that plants can be rotated, and groupings rearranged, so that the display is always at peak perfection. Tender plants can be moved to sheltered sites or indoors. (If this is impracticable, wrap the container in frost or shadecloth.)

Suitable containers

The small-space potagist has an enormous range of containers at his or her disposal, composed of wood, plastic, terracotta, concrete, wire, basketware and many other materials. Whatever it is made from, the container must be able to withstand frequent watering, be strong enough not to disintegrate during frequent moves and be complementary to the plants it displays as well as the garden site. Herbs and salad stuffs are often grown in window or built-in boxes which may be made of plastic or wood, though the latter can become very heavy when fully planted and wet. Most troughs for window boxes or rows of plantings should have a planting depth of at least 50–60 cm (20–24 in) to accommodate root growth.

The availability of jumbo-sized pots, crates and barrels in a variety of materials enables the container potagist to incorporate fruit trees into the planting scheme. Even inner-city dwellers can luxuriate in spring blossom and homegrown fruit from the wide variety of grafted and dwarf fruit trees available from good nurseries.

Grow-bags

Grow-bags are flattish polythene sacks of potting mix and compost with the addition of water-retention granules and slow-release fertiliser granules. They are designed to lay flat on the ground so that rows and blocks of plants or seedlings can be sown directly into them. To disguise the polythene, group smaller pots of companion plants such as marigolds, nasturtiums or herbs around the base. Grow-bags are excellent for the no-soil potager on a patio, veranda or rooftop since they can be disposed of when crops are finished and do not present storage problems as containers sometimes do.

Potting mixes

Success with all edible container plantings depends on the correct potting mix and moisturising agents. Most garden centres offer ready-mixed container mediums which include everything to promote plant health. Nutrients and slow-release fertiliser granules are readily available and the free-draining mix allows the soil around the roots to warm up quickly, promoting consistent healthy growth. Salad and leafy vegetables especially, need to grow quickly, as slow, stunted growth results in unpalatable, bitter-tasting crops.

Good quality ready-made mediums also contain water storage granules, a feature which has revolutionised the art of container gardening by minimising the time and labour formerly spent hand watering. The granules are marketed under names such as 'Crystal' or 'Liquid Rain' and when mixed with water swell up to many times their normal size. They work on the principle of retaining moisture so that plant roots penetrating the jelly-like granules extract moisture as they require it. The crystals swell anew each time the container is watered. Manufacturers also offer a product generally marketed as

There is maximum use of space in this small thriving edible garden. Fruit trees are espaliered, a wire frame provides support for vertical plantings, the raised beds feature broccoli with bold silver-blue foliage to the right, and broad beans flank a handsome Burrelli pot. A cold frame for raising seedlings is backed with the bold foliage and golden flowers of zucchini plants, and a small stone duck tucked away at the rear right provides a pleasant touch of whimsy.

'Slippery Water' for ease of re-wetting dry mix and ensuring fast and even water penetration.

Also widely available are clay-based products for reducing moisture loss from containers of terracotta and stone. The substance is painted onto the inside lining of the pots, and a small hole left at the base to allow excess water to drain away.

It is more economical to buy potting mix and compost in bulk and bag it up in bin sacks if you are unable to make your own. If storage is a problem, the best option is to grow your edibles in grow-bags containing ready-mix. These may be stacked vertically until required and take up relatively little space.

If you are able to make your own potting mix, it should be sandy and porous but still able to hold moisture. Slow-release fertiliser and water-retention granules should be added. A good homemade mixture is two parts well manured and conditioned garden soil, one part coarse sand and one part garden compost, and

An innovative edible garden in a tiny courtyard. Climbing beans scramble up a small trellis, beet, salad stuffs and herbs are tucked into tiered planter boxes between the benches and citrus are grown in terracotta pots: living proof, literally, that fruit, herbs, flowers and vegetables may be grown in 'no soil' situations on patios and decks, in courtyards or even on rooftops.

peat moss or a moisture-retaining agent such as vermiculite. Add 30 g (1 oz) of complete fertiliser (NKP 5:7:4) and 100 g (3 oz) of lime to each bucket of mix and mix all components well.

Successive planting and repotting

Keep extra containers on hand so that new seedlings will be developing to replace crops which are being harvested. If storage space is short, use polythene planter bags which squash flat when not in use. It is possible to recycle the old mix from finished crops but it should be treated before being used again. Add commercially prepared compost, slow-release fertiliser granules and water-retaining granules, but if you do not wish to mix your own, garden centres offer several commercially prepared agents for revitalising used potting mix.

The flat-dweller's guide to composting

With the following method, you can make compost in a very small area or in a well-ventilated corner of a shed or garage. The key to success with this method lies in plentiful aeration and the addition of soil-based materials such as discarded potting mixes from containers. If you can beg, borrow or steal a few bags of garden soil containing some worms this will give you a head start. Worms will work and aerate the organic materials for you and their castings are the earth's best fertiliser. They will soon multiply, and as you use the matured compost, set portions containing worms aside in a separate container. This will ensure you can always top up a new brew. The container for the mini-worm farm should contain plenty of aeration holes, be covered against mice, rats and birds and stored in a cool dark place.

You can make your compost in any old container as long as you drill plenty of aeration holes first. A wooden box is best, but plastic will do as long as holes are pierced in the base for drainage and up and down all sides for aeration. Raise the container just above the ground by standing it on blocks of wood or half-bricks. Fill it in layers with chopped roots, stalks and foliage of any spent crops, all organic kitchen waste – fruit and vegetable peelings (avoid cooked food scraps which may attract vermin and cause unpleasant odours), tea bags, used coffee grounds – the contents of vacuum cleaner bags, shrubby and coarse prunings to help with aeration, and discarded potting mixes from containers. Do not add any liquids, such as the contents of tea or coffee pots, as they will make the mix unduly damp causing it to become an unusable, wet, smelly mess. Add sprinklings of complete fertiliser or commercially-prepared manure pellets between layers. Cover the mixture lightly and let it lie for a month or so (turn it once weekly) until the organic materials rot into compost.

If you stand a container beneath the drainage holes at the base to catch seepage, this may be diluted with water to make liquid manure.

Liquid feeds and fertilisers

A good new potting mix or well manured and conditioned soil should provide your vegetables with all the nutrients they need, but crops in containers require frequent watering and nutrients wash out of the mix quite quickly. These can be replaced with water-soluble fertilisers every fortnight or so, and most plants benefit from a booster foliar feed, especially at the time of flowering. There are a wide variety of foliar fertilisers readily available. Instructions per rate of dilution and application are clearly given on the packaging.

The manufacturers of many commercially prepared foliar fertilisers offer a 'Feeder Set' which contains a pack of plant food, a clip-on hose connector and a feeder jar. There is no mess or complicated mixing; the handy feeder jar is clipped straight onto the end of the ordinary garden hose and the plants are fed and watered

at the same time. Foliar fertilisers should, however, be used only as booster feeds, the plants' main nutrition coming from well fed, well conditioned soil. Take care with preparations which are high in nitrogenous minerals – these are fine for leafy vegetables, but will promote lush foliage at the expense of flowers in fruiting varieties. There are also products which come as slow-release fertiliser granules. Sprinkled into containers, they release nutrients over a period of about nine months.

Horticultural suppliers also offer a comprehensive range of organic fertilisers such as seaweed-based liquid plant foods for fern and foliage, flower and fruit, general purpose, rose formula, super organic blend, super seaweed, and blood and bone formula. Another good organic foliar feed is a concentrated fish fertiliser. I use this particular variety because the smell deters pests, and it is not too high in nitrogen. These products are excellent aids to container cultivation, and may of course be used in any garden situation. All things considered, there is no excuse for fruit and vegetables grown in no-soil situations and tiny spaces not to come up smiling with rude good health and fruit prolifically!

The raised vegetable bed in this unusual small potager rejoices in a fragrant framework of pink and white lavenders and thyme. The no-mow fragrant thyme lawn, *Thymus* 'Snowdrift', is bordered on the left with the striking lime-green flowers of *Alchemilla mollis* and to the front with plantings of mint, lavender and thyme in weathered terracotta containers.

Above: This highly productive small potager is tucked into a small area beneath the decking of the house. The bed is planted to the left with onions, broccoli, capsicums and celery, and to the right with tomatoes, capsicums, basil, chives, potatoes and petunias.
Opposite: Circles and paths of mellow bricks have been used to create a formal design in this small potager. Box-edged strawberry beds are netted to deter avian visitors!

Topiary and standardised plants

Containerised topiary specimens are invaluable for lending elegance and symmetry to the small-space potager and enhance its basically formal structure. Smaller shrubs and ornamentals have been containerised and trained as topiary specimens and standards for many centuries. To the novice potagist, the art of pruning to shape topiary specimens appears to be a somewhat technical and on occasion dangerous horticultural skill to master. Those elegant standards are also exorbitantly expensive from the nursery, which is always a compelling reason to try one's own hand. It is reassuring to remember in the learning stages that very few plants will die as the result of incorrect pruning. At worst, your specimen may not produce any flowers or fruit for a season or two, but it will certainly survive!

However, it is as well to be aware that not all shrubs and trees make successful subjects for topiary. Some cannot tolerate severe cutting, eventually losing their vigour. Others grow much too quickly so that they become labour intensive, others produce foliage that is too open to allow any impression of shape. The species which follow suffer from none of these

drawbacks. They are generally slow-growing and densely leaved, and will respond to trimming by producing new shoots each year.

English box (*Buxus sempervirens*) and yew (*Taxus* spp.) are the traditional shrubs for topiary, but they are slow to mature, and the latter can grow very large. *Lonicera nitida* will shape every bit as well as box and in half the time. Holly trees (*Ilex* spp.) with glossy (and somewhat prickly) leaves are ideal for clipping into simple shapes. Many of the larger thuja conifers (*Thuja* spp.) train into stout hedges and will also prune well to simple geometric shapes.

Topiary is an ancient art, and one which is gaining considerable interest from modern gardeners. The more complicated shapes do take more skill since they involve plants trained over wire frames, and one must, as the saying goes, possess one's soul in patience while the plants grow. For the modern potagist a steady hand and just a little patience is all that is required in learning how to develop plant sculptures. It can take many years to develop an impressive geometric head on a tall stem but, when in a hurry – cheat!

From the nursery choose a suitable tree or shrub (preferably two, for symmetry) with a strong, straight central trunk and a full, well developed head. Remove all the lower branches to the height you desire, and then trim the head lightly to a chosen shape. For the beginner topiarist it is wise to stick to simple geometric shapes such as balls, cubes, columns and triangles, and a couple of passable topiary standards may be shaped in a few hours instead of years. You can experiment with advanced shapes on frames when you have gained experience.

It may be wise to provide a strong stake for taller standards, because the density of their heads can make them a little top heavy and susceptible to strong winds. Use soft ties so that the trunk does not suffer injury. Any new growth shoots which appear on the trunk should be promptly removed, and new growth on the head should be pinched back regularly to encourage even more shoots. This growth pro-

vides the density of foliage you require to train into a desired shape.

Other traditional shrubs which make attractive standard plants or topiary specimens include roses, conifers, camellias and bay trees (*Laurus nobilis*), upright rosemary (*Rosmarinus officinalis*), lavender varieties (especially *Lavandula dentata*, which has strong upright growth and is quick growing), citrus, orange blossom (*Philadelphus coronaria*) and hydrangeas. Many more small trees and shrubs clip well into simple forms and, in addition to providing vertical accents and focal points, they are highly ornamental, take little space and lend grace and dignity to the potager. Above all, they are well suited to life in containers.

Cultivating the small-space potager

Exactly the same rules apply as for the huge-space potager! Intensive vegetable production in a tiny area requires beds of well conditioned soil which has been enriched with organic manures and materials. Dense planting provides ground-cover to maximise moisture retention and vertical planting maximises ground space for vegetables of a more terrestrial habit. Choose a sunny, sheltered site. Plan for continuity of produce by setting aside space for a nursery area for young plants to replace those which have been harvested. Sow catch crops between larger varieties and practise crop rotation and the appropriate organic management principles set out in Chapter 8.

CHAPTER 7

QUICK REFERENCE GUIDES

Quick reference guide to planting design

This summary of ideas for planting design is by no means exhaustive. The individual gardener will have many ideas of his or her own, and it is to be remembered that the plants suggested will perform according to geographical locations and climatic conditions.

Edgers for outlining beds and parterres

Edgers and dividers may be designed in a semi-permanent capacity as annual crops and flowers, or in a permanent capacity as perennial shrubs, herbs, hedges, espaliered fruits and vines, dwarf trees or soft-fruit bushes.

Low edgers – annuals: dwarf red basils, beetroot, dwarf marigolds and nasturtiums, ornamental kales, coloured lettuce, oriental brassicas of the 'cut and come again' varieties, dwarf annual bedding dahlias and zinnias, strawberries. **Perennials**: cottage pinks, catmint, chives, bush thymes and sages, violas, violets, dwarf feverfew, lady's mantle (*Alchemilla mollis*), dwarf lavenders.

Medium edgers – annuals: taller varieties of basil, bush beans, beetroot, red cabbage, bedding dahlias and zinnias, pot marigolds, summer savory, phacelia, celery, beetroot, rainbow beet or chard. **Perennials**: lemon balm (*Melissa officinalis*), lavenders, box, *Lonicera nitida*, sages, winter savory (*Satureja montana*), rosemary, santolina and artemisias.

Tall edgers – annuals: broccoli, cauliflower, cosmos, lavatera, sunflowers, amaranths, sweetcorn, taller marigolds, frames and trellises of sweet peas, peas and beans. **Perennials**: dahlias, dwarf hebes, French lavender (*Lavandula denticulata*), rosemary, rue, santolina, *Sedum spectabile*, and ancient rugosa roses which have beautifully scented flowers and highly ornamental hips, also the apothecary's rose *Rosa gallica officinalis*. Soft-fruit bushes, espaliered fruit, standard roses, rosemary, lavender or bay, and topiary specimens.

Vertical accents

For overall balance the potager requires plant groupings of varying heights. A selection of herbs, vegetables and flowers to add vertical accent might include:

Without support: amaranths, angelica, artichokes, asparagus, bay laurel, sweetcorn, delphiniums, many brassicas, canna lilies, cardoons, clary sage (*Salvia sclarea*), larkspur, green and bronze fennel, hollyhocks, horseradish, lemon verbena, *Phlomis samia*, standard roses, fruit bushes and topiary specimens, rosemary, rhubarb, ornamental tobaccos (*Nicotiana* spp.), verbascums, borage.

Needing support: runner beans, peas, cucurbits on trellises, tomatoes, espaliered or cordon fruit trees, climbing nasturtiums and sweet peas, grape and passion fruit vines, honeysuckle, climbing roses and sunflowers.

Plants having strong design for architectural accents

Artichokes, broccoli, cauliflowers, canna lilies, cardoons, sweetcorn, cucurbits trained to climb, bronze fennel, angelica, ornamental kales, sweet and hot peppers, rhubarb, rue, artemisias, *Sedum spectabile*, sunflowers, beefsteak tomato cultivars, borage.

Bushy or clump-forming hedging and evergreen plants

Box (*Buxus sempervirens*), *Lonicera nitida*, curry plant (*Helichrysum*), silver germander

(*Teucrium fruticans*), dwarf hebes, bay laurel, hyssop, lavenders, rosemary, rue, winter savory, bush thymes and sages, santolina.

Foliage favourites
Feathery: asparagus, carrots, dill, cumin and fennel. **Curly**: curly endive, parsley and kale.

Self-sowers
Borage, chervil, cosmos, evening primrose, fennel, feverfew, hollyhocks, lettuces, marigolds, nasturtiums, Californian poppies (*Eschscholzia* spp.), mustard, nicotiana, oregano, phacelia, violas, catmint, lady's mantle (*Alchemilla mollis*).

Fast fillers
Gratifyingly quick plants and crops to mature include oriental brassicas, dwarf beans, feverfew, chervil, cosmos, land cress, mustard, phacelia, salad transplants and bedding plants such as annual marigolds, dahlias, zinnias and nasturtiums.

A palette of vegetable, flower and herb colours
Red, purple or violet-blue – Amaranths, aubergines/eggplants, purple basils, red Brussels sprouts, broccoli, cabbages, kales, kohlrabi, lettuces, red chicory, bronze mustard, red orache, purple-leafed sage, sweet peppers and chillies, tomatoes, beetroot, purple-podded climbing beans, bedding dahlias with purple-black foliage, zinnias, roses and nasturtiums, strawberries, raspberries, blackberries, blueberries, gooseberries, the flowers of artichoke and cardoons, rainbow beet, runner beans, borage, lavender, purple-flowered peas, catmint, phacelia and chicory flowers.

Pink tones – True pink is an unusual colour amongst edible plants, which is a matter for regret since it is an excellent foil to the rich greens of vegetable foliage. Appropriate plants offering pink hues might include roses, ornamental kales, pink, cream and green splashed tricolour sage, the flowers of common marjoram, oregano and thyme species, Chinese artichokes, some dwarf beans, the seed globes of leeks (pale pink), and flowers such as dahlias and zinnias – all subject of course to the usual seasonal fluctuations.

Yellow and gold tones – Yellow-leafed varieties of lemon balm, oregano, celery, rainbow beet and garden sages; the fruit of butter beans, peppers and chillies, the flowers and fruit of squash, pumpkins, courgettes/zucchini and other cucurbits, some tomatoes; the flowers of brassicas, sunflowers, zinnias, bedding dahlias, nasturtiums and marigolds.

Silver and white – Artemisias, artichokes, cardoons, curry plant, lavenders, santolina, cauliflowers, white aubergines, Chinese chives, white kohlrabi, turnips, leeks, radish. Broad beans provide silver-green foliage and black and white flowers; many bean and pea cultivars offer white flowers, as do potatoes and white lavender. Onions, garlic, and chives also provide the foil of silver-green foliage.

It is possible and fun to experiment with all sorts of floral, fruit and vegetable permutations, but it is wise to find out which flowers are invasive through self-sowing to avoid unfair competition with the edibles!

The quick reference guides that follow are designed to give the potagist immediate information regarding the life cycle, hardiness and colour of edible plants including vegetables, fruit, nuts, flowers and herbs. Information is given on whether support is required and on correct siting. Space does not allow for extensive individual cultivation details, and it is assumed that unless stated otherwise, all edible plants require a humus-enriched, moist but well draining soil in a position of full sun.

TABLE 1: Vegetable growth guide

Plant	Lifetime	Hardiness	Site	Height	Spread	Support
AMARANTHUS	A	T	FS	T	M	M
ASPARAGUS	P	H	T	T	W	Y
ASPARAGUS PEA	A	T	FS	L	N	N
AUBERGINE/EGGPLANT	A	VT	FS	M	M	Y
BEANS, BROAD	A	H	T	M	N	N
BEANS, DWARF	A	T	T	L	N	N
BEANS, CLIMBING	A*	T	T	C	N	C
BEANS, HYACINTH	A	VT	FS	C	N	C
BEANS, SOYA	A	VT	FS	L	N	N
BEETROOT	B	H	T	L	N	N
BROCCOLI	A	VH	T	M	M	M
BRUSSELS SPROUTS	A	VH	T	M	M	M
BURDOCK	P	VH	T	M	W	N
CABBAGE	A	VH	T	M	M	M
CAPSICUM	A	VH	FS	M	M	M
CARDOON	P	H	T	VT	W	M
CARROT	B	H	T	L	N	N
CAULIFLOWER	A	VH	T	M	M	M
CELERIAC	A	H	T	L	N	N
CELERY	A	VH	T	L	N	N
CHARD	B	H	T	M	M	N
CHICORY	P	T	T	L	N	N
CHINESE ARTICHOKE	P	H	T	L	N	N
CHINESE BRASSICAS	A	VARY	T	VARY	VARY	
CHOP-SUEY GREENS	A	H	T	T	N	N
CLAYTONIA	A	H	T	VL	N	N
CORN SALAD	A	H	T	VL	N	N
COURGETTE/ZUCCHINI	A	VT	T	M	W	N
CRESS, GARDEN	A	T	T	VL	VN	N
CRESS, LAND	B	H	T	VL	N	N
CRESS, WATER	P	H	T	VL	N	N
DANDELION	P	VH	T	VL	N	N
ENDIVE	P	T	T	VL	N	N
FENNEL	A	T	FS	M	M	N
GARLIC	A*	H	T	L	VN	N
GLOBE ARTICHOKE	P	H	FS	M	M	N
GOOD KING HENRY	P	VH	T	L	N	N
HAMBURG PARSLEY	B	H	T	L	N	N
HOPS	P	VH	T	C	W	C
ICEPLANT	A	VT	FS	L	M	N
JERUSALEM ARTICHOKE	P	VH	T	VT	M	M
KALE	A	VH	T	M	M	M
KOHLRABI	A	H	T	L	N	N
LEEK	A	VH	T	L	VN	N
LETTUCE	A	T	T	VL	N	N
MAIZE	A	VT	FS	T	M	M
MARROW	A	VT	T	M	VW	N
NEW ZEALAND SPINACH	A	T	T	L	N	N
OKRA	A	VT	FS	M	M	N
ONION	B	H	T	L	N	N
ORACHE	A	H	T	T	M	M
PARSNIP	B	VH	T	L	N	N
PEAS	A	T	T	VARY	N	C
POTATO	A*	H	T	L	W	N
PUMPKIN	A	VT	T	M	VW	N
PURSLANE	A	VT	T	L	VN	N
QUINOA	A	T	T	T	N	N
RADISH	A	H	T	VL	VN	N
ROCKET	A	H	T	L	N	N
SALSIFY	A	H	T	L	N	N
SCORZONERA	P	H	T	L	N	N
SEAKALE	P	H	T	M	M	N
SHALLOT	B	T	T	L	N	N
SKIRRET	P	H	T	T	M	M
SORREL	P	VH	T	L	N	N
SPINACH	A	T	T	L	N	N
SQUASH	A	VT	T	M	VW	N
SWEDE	A	H	T	L	N	N
SWEETCORN	A	VT	FS	T	M	M
SUNFLOWER	A	T	FS	VT	W	Y
TOMATO	A	VT	FS	M	M	Y
TURNIP	A	VH	T	L	N	N
WHEAT	A	H	T	M	N	N

Lifetime
A Annual, from seed to seed in one season
A* Treat as annual
B Biennial, from seed to seed in two seasons
P Perennial, plant lives many years

Hardiness
VT Very Tender, will not tolerate any frost
T Tender, will tolerate slight frost if protected
H Hardy, will tolerate some frost
VH Very Hardy, will stand severe frost

Site
FS Full Sum
T Tolerant

Height
VT Very Tall, over 2 m (78 in)
T Tall, 1–2 m (36–78 in)
M Medium, 50–100 cm (18–36 in)
L Low, 15–50 cm (6–18 in)
VL Very Low, under 15 cm (6 in)

Spread
VW Very Wide, over 2 m (78 in)
W Wide, 1–2 m (36–78 in)
M Medium, 50–100 cm (18–36 in)
N Narrow, 15–50 cm (6–18 in)
VN Very Narrow, under 15 cm (6 in)

Support
Y Yes
N Not needed
C Climber
M May be needed on windy site

TABLE 2: Vegetable colour guide I

Vegetables	Leaves GREEN				Silvery	Leaves RED		Leaves PURPLE	Leaves YELLOW	Stem				
	Dark	Medium	Pale	Variegated	Silvery	Dark	Greeny-Red	Greeny-Purple	Yellowy-Green	Green	Red	Purple	Yellow	White
AMARANTHUS	Y					Y			Y	Y	Y			
ASPARAGUS		Y												
ASPARAGUS PEA	Y									Y				
AUBERGINE/EGGPLANT										Y				
BEANS, BROAD			Y							Y				
BEANS, CLIMBING		Y						Y	Y	Y		Y	Y	
BEANS, DWARF		Y						Y	Y	Y		Y		
BEANS, HYACINTH		Y						Y						
BEANS, SOYA			Y											
BEETROOT		Y				Y	Y			Y	Y		Y	
BROCCOLI		Y								Y				
BRUSSELS SPROUTS		Y				Y	Y			Y				
BURDOCK				Y										
CABBAGE		Y	Y			Y								
CAPSICUM		Y												
CARDOON					Y									
CARROT		Y												
CAULIFLOWER			Y											
CELERIAC	Y													
CELERY		Y							Y					
CHARD		Y				Y	Y				Y		Y	
CHICORY		Y				Y								Y
CHINESE ARTICHOKE		Y												
CHINESE BRASSICAS	VARY													
CHOP-SUEY GREENS		Y												
CLAYTONIA		Y												
CORN SALAD		Y												
COURGETTE/ZUCCHINI				Y					Y					
CRESS, GARDEN		Y												
CRESS, LAND		Y		Y										
CRESS, WATER		Y												
DANDELION		Y												
ENDIVE			Y											
FENNEL			Y											
GARLIC			Y											
GLOBE ARTICHOKE					Y									
GOOD KING HENRY	Y													
HAMBURG PARSLEY		Y												
HOPS		Y	Y						Y					
ICEPLANT					Y									
JERUSALEM ARTICHOKE		Y								Y				
KALE	Y	Y	Y	Y		Y	Y	Y		Y		Y		
KOHLRABI		Y						Y		Y		Y		
LEEK		Y						Y						
LETTUCE			Y	Y		Y	Y							
MAIZE		Y												
MARROW		Y		Y	Y									
NZ SPINACH		Y												
OKRA		Y				Y								
ONION		Y			Y									
ORACHE						Y			Y	Y		Y		
PARSNIP		Y												
PEAS		Y												
POTATO		Y												
PUMPKIN		Y												
PURSLANE		Y							Y					
QUINOA		Y												
RADISH		Y												
ROCKET		Y												
SALSIFY		Y												
SCORZONERA		Y												
SEAKALE	T													
SHALLOT		Y	Y											
SKIRRET		Y												
SORREL		Y								Y				
SPINACH		Y												
SQUASH		Y												
SWEDE		Y												
SWEETCORN		Y		Y										
SUNFLOWER		Y								Y				
TOMATO		Y												
TURNIP		Y												
WHEAT					Y									

TABLE 3: Vegetable colour guide II

Vegetables with no significant flowers or fruit have been omitted from this table.

Vegetables	Flowers						Fruit					
	Red	Pink	Yellow	Blue	Purple	White	Red	Pink	Yellow	Purple	White	Green
AMARANTHUS	Y		Y				Y					
ASPARAGUS							Y			Y		
ASPARAGUS PEA	Y				Y							Y
AUBERGINE/EGGPLANT			Y	Y						Y		
BEANS, BROAD	Y					Y						Y
BEANS, CLIMBING	Y				Y	Y	Y	Y		Y		Y
BEANS, DWARF	Y	Y			Y	Y	Y		Y	Y		Y
BEANS, HYACINTH						Y						Y
BEANS, SOYA					Y	Y	Y			Y		Y
BEETROOT										Y		
BROCCOLI			Y							Y		Y
BRUSSELS SPROUTS			Y					Y		Y		Y
BURDOCK												
CABBAGE			Y									
CAPSICUM							Y	Y	Y	Y		Y
CARDOON					Y					Y		Y
CARROT						Y						
CAULIFLOWER			Y									
CHICORY				Y								
CHINESE ARTICHOKE		Y										
CHINESE BRASSICAS			Y		Y							
CHOP-SUEY GREENS			Y									
CLAYTONIA						Y						
CORN SALAD				Y								
COURGETTE/ZUCCHINI			Y						Y			Y
CRESS, WATER			Y									
DANDELION			Y									
ENDIVE				Y								
FENNEL			Y									
GARLIC					Y							
GLOBE ARTICHOKE					Y							
HOPS												Y
JERUSALEM ARTICHOKE			Y									
KALE			Y									
KOHLRABI			Y									
LEEK					Y	Y						
MAIZE							Y		Y	Y	Y	
MARROW			Y						Y	Y	Y	Y
NZ SPINACH												
OKRA			Y				Y					Y
PEAS		Y				Y				Y		Y
POTATO					Y	Y						
PUMPKIN			Y						Y			Y
QUINOA							Y	Y	Y	Y	Y	
RADISH							Y					Y
ROCKET							Y					
SALSIFY					Y							
SCORZONERA			Y									
SEAKALE							Y					
SKIRRET							Y					
SORREL	Y											
SPINACH												
SQUASH			Y						Y			Y
SWEDE												
SWEETCORN							Y		Y		Y	
SUNFLOWER			Y									
TOMATO			Y				Y		Y			
WHEAT			Y							Y		

TABLE 4: Useful flowers guide

Common Name	Latin Name	Edible	Bee/Butterfly Attractor	Predator Attractor	Pest Repellant	Pest Attractor	Green Manure
ALFALFA/LUCERNE	Medicago sativa						Y
ANISE HYSSOP	Agastache foeniculum	Y	Y				
BABY BLUE EYES	Nemophila insignis		Y	Y			
BASIL	Ocimum basilicum	Y					
BERGAMOT	Monarda didyma	Y	Y				
BLUE LUPIN	Lupinus angustifolius		Y				Y
BORAGE	Borago officinalis	Y	Y			Y	
BUCKWHEAT	Fagopyrum esculentum						Y
CALENDULA	Calendula officinalis	Y	Y	Y		Y	
CHERVIL	Anthriscum cerefolium	Y					

TABLE 4: Useful flowers guide (continued)

Common Name	Latin Name	Edible	Bee/Butterfly Attractor	Predator Attractor	Pest Repellant	Pest Attractor	Green Manure
CHICORY	Cichorium intybus	Y	Y				
CHIVE	Allium schoenoprasum	Y			Y		
CHOP-SUEY GREENS	Chrysanthemum coronarium	Y	Y				
CHRYSANTHEMUM	Chrysanthemum x morifolium	Y					
CORIANDER	Coriandrum sativum	Y		Y			
COWSLIP	Primula veris	Y					
CRIMSON CLOVER	Trifolium incarnatum	Y	Y				Y
DAISY	Bellis perennis	Y	Y				
DAYLILY	Hemerocallis fulva	Y	Y				
DILL	Anethum graveolens	Y					
ELDER	Sambucus nigra	Y			Y	Y	
FENNEL	Foeniculum vulgare	Y					
FENUGREEK	Trigonella foenum graecum						Y
FIELD BEANS	Vicia faba		Y				
GARLIC CHIVE	Allium tuberosum	Y			Y		
GRAZING RYE	Secale cereale						Y
HOLLYHOCK	Alcea rosea	Y	Y				
HONEYSUCKLE	Lonicera japonica	Y	Y				
LAVENDER	Lavandula angustifolia	Y	Y		Y		
LEMON	Citrus limon	Y					
LEMON BALM	Melissa officinalis	Y					
LILAC	Syringa vulgaris	Y	Y				
LOVAGE	Levisticum officinale	Y					
MARIGOLD FRENCH	Tagetes patula		Y		Y		
MARIGOLD MEXICAN	Tagetes minuta		Y		Y		
MARJORAM	Origanum majorana	Y	Y				
MEDDICK	Medicago lupulina						Y
MINT	Mentha spp.	Y					
MUSTARD	Sinapsis alba		Y	Y	Y		Y
NASTURTIUM	Tropaeolum majus	Y	Y			Y	
ORANGE	Citrus sinensis	Y					
OREGANO	Origanum spp.	Y	Y				
PHACELIA	Phacelia tanacetifolia		Y	Y			Y
PINK	Dianthus spp.	Y	Y				
POACHED-EGG PLANT	Limnanthes douglasii		Y	Y			
PRIMROSE	Primula vulgaris	Y					
RED CLOVER	Trifolium pratense	Y	Y				Y
ROCKET	Eruca vesicaria	Y					
ROSE	Rosa spp.	Y	Y			Y	
ROSEMARY	Rosmarinus officinalis	Y	Y		Y		
SAGE	Salvia officinalis	Y	Y				
SAVORY, SUMMER	Satureja hortensis	Y					
SAVORY, WINTER	Satureja montana	Y					
SCENTED GERANIUM	Pelargonium spp.	Y					
SQUASH	Cucurbita spp.	Y	Y				
TANSY	Tanacetum vulgare		Y	Y	Y		
TARES	Vicia sativa						Y
THYME	Thymus spp.	Y	Y				
TULIP	Tulipa spp.	Y	Y				
VIOLA	Viola odorata, V. x wittrockiana	Y	Y				

TABLE 5: Fruit and nut growth

Name	Height	Spread	Hardiness	Training						
				Fine	Bush	Standard	Espalier	Fan	Cordon	Tunnel
ALMOND	T	VW	H			Y				
APPLE	T/VT	VW	VH			Y	Y	Y	Y	Y
APRICOT	VT	VW	H			Y	Y	Y		
BLACKBERRY	VT	VW	VH	Y						Y
BLACKBERRY HYBRIDS	VT	VW	H	Y						Y
BLACKCURRANT	M	M	H		Y					
BLUEBERRY	M	M	VH		Y					
CHERRY	T/VT	VW	VH			Y	Y	Y		
CHESTNUT	VVT	VW	V							
CRAB APPLE	T/VT	VW	VH			Y				Y
ELDER	VT	VW	VH		Y					
FIG	VT	VW	H		Y			Y		
GOOSEBERRY	M	M	H		Y		Y			
GRAPE	VT	VW	H	Y						Y
HAZEL	VT	VW	VH		Y					Y
HUCKLEBERRY	M	N	ANN							
KIWI	VT	VW	T	Y						Y
LEMON	T	VW	T			Y				
MEDLAR	VT	VW	VH			Y	Y			

TABLE 5: Fruit and nut growth (continued)

				Training						
MELON	L	W	VT	Y						
MULBERRY	VVT	VW	VH			Y	Y			Y
NECTARINE	VT	VW	H			Y	Y	Y		
ORANGE	T	VW	T			Y				
PASSIONFRUIT	VT	VW	H	Y						Y
PEACH	VT	VW	H			Y	Y	Y		
PEAR	T/VT	VW	VH			Y	Y	Y	Y	Y
PHYSALIS	T	N	ANN							
PLUM	T/VT	VW	VH			Y	Y	Y		
QUINCE	VT	VW	VH			Y	Y			Y
RASPBERRY	T	M	VH	Y						
RED/WHITECURRANT	M	M	H		Y	Y				
RHUBARB	M	W	VH							
STRAWBERRY	VL	N	H							
WALNUT	VVT	VW	VH							
WINEBERRY	T	M	VH	Y						Y

TABLE 6: Oriental vegetable reference chart

English catalogue	Botanical name	Chinese or Japanese name	Other names
Amaranth, vegetable	Amaranthus gangenticus	Hinn Choy-Shien-(hiyu)	Chinese spinach, callaloo, bayam
Broccoli, Chinese	Brassica alboglabra	Gai-Lohn, Kai laan, Fat Shan	Chinese kale
Cabbage, Chinese	Brassica oleracea	Yeh choy	
Cabbage, Swatow mustard	Brassica juncea	Daai gaai choi, Gai Choy	Indian mustard, mustard green
Cabbage, Santoh frilled	Brassica pekinensis	Yokyo Bekana	open celery cabbage
Cabbage, Santoh round leaf	Brassica pekinensis	Maruba Santoh	open celery cabbage
Cabbage, Tah Tsai	Brassica chinensis	Taai goo choy	non-heading Chinese cabbage, Chinese flat cabbage
Celtuce	Lactuca sativa asparagina	Woh sun	stem lettuce
Celery, Chinese	Apium graveolens	Kunn choi, Kintsai	Heung Kunn
Chives, garlic	Allium tuberosum odoratum	Gow choi — Nira	Chinese chives, Chinese leek
Coriander/Cilantro	Coriandrum sativum	Yuen sai — Enshui	Chinese parsley, Dhania
Cress, water	Nasturtium officinale	Sai yeung choy	
Cucumber, Oriental	Cucumus sativus	Kee chi, Tseng gwa	
Eggplant, Japanese	Solanum melogena	Ai gwa	aubergine
Gourd, bottle	Lagenaria siceraria	Woo lo gwa	
Gourd, vegetable	Cucurbito pepo		
Komatsuna	Brassica campestris		mustard spinach
Malabar spinach	Basella rubra	Saan choy	Ceylon spinach, slippery vegetable
Melon, bitter	Momordica charantia	Foo gwa	balsam pear
Melon, Chinese winter	Benincasa hispada	Too-gwa, Dong-gwa	white or wax gourd, ash melon
Melon, fuzzy	Benincasa hispada	Tseet gwa, Mao gwa	little winter melon
Mibuna	Brassica rapa	Ren sheng cai	Mibu greens
Mitsuba	Cryptotaenia japonica	San ye gin	Japanese parsley trefoil, Japanese honeywort
Mizuna	Brassica japonica	Shui tsai	Chinese mustard pot herb, Japanese mustard/lettuce
Mustard, Mike giant purple	Brassica rapa	Mike Ta Kona	mustard greens
Mustard, giant red	Brassica rapa	Aka takena	mustard greens
Mustard, green in snow	Brassica juncea	Xue li hang serifang	leaf mustard
Mustard, spinach	Brassica rapa perviridis	Komatsuna	
Okra, Chinese	Luffa acutangula	Cee gwa	angled luffa
Onion, bunching white Welsh	Allium fistulosum	Chang fa nebuka	bunching onion, scallions, cibol
Pak Choi	Brassica chinensis	Bok choi, Baak cho	Chinese white cabbage
Pak Choi, flowering	Brassica parachinensis	Tsai shim, Choy sum	Chinese flowering cabbage
Pak Choi, flowering purple	Brassica parachinensis	Hon tsai tai	Chinese flowering cabbage
Pea, snow	Pisum sativum	Ho lon dow	edible podded peas
Peppers, hot	Capsicum frutescens	La chiao Laat jiu	chilli pepper
Peppers, sweet	Capsicum annum	Tseng jiu	
Perilla, green	Perilla frutescens	Jisoo-Ao shisho	beefstake plant/summer coleus
Perilla, red	Perilla frutescens	Jisoo-Ao shisho	beefstake plant/summer coleus
Radish, Chinese	Raphanus sativus	Loh baak	Mullangi (India)
Radish, Japanese	Raphanus acanthiformis	Diakon	Chinese turnip
Shungiku	Chrysanthemum coronarium	Shingiku	Chop Suey green, garland chrysanthemum
Senposai	Brassica spp.		Japanese spinach
Spinach	Spinacia oleracea		
Squash, spaghetti	Cucurbita pepo		vegetable spaghetti
Turnip	Brassica rapa var. glabra	Pai lo po	
Water spinach	Ipomoea aquatica	Ong chov-Entsai	water convolvulus

CHAPTER 8

ORGANIC MANAGEMENT

The organic gardener's philosophy

The organic gardener believes that toxic pesticides and herbicides are harmful to the environment, to plant and animal life, and that they poison nature's food chains. In adopting this philosophy, he or she avoids non-specific chemical treatments (indiscriminate killing power) and uses alternative methods of pest, disease and weed control. These either attempt to follow nature's own controls or are designed to eliminate only the unwanted pests or plants. The aim is to grow as wide a diversity of plants as possible without employing toxic chemicals.

Chemical pesticides are specifically designed to kill. Some act on the nervous system of insects and some affect the digestive system. Whatever they do, they are all *poisons* and present just as much danger to human beings. Chemical companies claim toxic chemicals are all rigorously tested and are used in such weak dilutions that they do not pose a risk to people. They then go on to instruct on the huge amount of protective clothing one must wear before using these preparations – goggles, masks, rubber gloves, impermeable spraysuits and sometimes even breathing equipment . . .

The organic gardener wants to share his or her potager with a myriad of birds, bees, butterflies and insects, and eat spray-free food. He or she cannot do this if everything is smothered in broad spectrum toxic insecticides.

Principles of organic management

The key to the total organic management of my large garden has evolved through experience and a combination of the following principles:

1. The use of insecticide, fungicide and herbicides made from non-chemical organic materials, i.e., plant derivatives such as garlic and pyrethrum concentrates.

2. Awareness of the fact that even organic pesticides if applied at incorrect strength, or at the wrong time of day, can kill beneficial insects as well as pests.

3. The growing of disease-resistant plant varieties so that the need for spraying is minimised, and the discarding of disease-prone species. The growing of plants well suited to one's individual soil and climatic conditions and avoidance of those for which artificial cultivation conditions must be created.

4. Employment of companion planting in conjunction with non-toxic sprays to attract beneficial insects and repel undesirable ones in specific areas.

5. The avoidance of monoculture which attracts large numbers of specific insect pests in one area. Plants set in clumps or rows of different species both attract and repel specific insects, ensuring a natural balance between the two. In medieval days (before chemical sprays), gardeners did not differentiate between plants at all. A plant was a plant whether you ate it, smelt it or simply enjoyed its beauty, and they were all grown together.

6. Provision of plant hosts on which beneficial insects may breed or feed – a biological 'bug eat bug' method of control by encouraging natural predators which prey on pests.

7. Acceptance of a tolerable measure of disease and pests in the garden controlled by organic methods, rather than a pest and disease-free garden achieved by the use of non-specific chemicals.

Planted in well fed, well conditioned soil, climbing beans and apple cucumbers promise prolific crops to come. The beds are heavily mulched with straw to ensure moisture retention, and when broken down as the beds are worked, this mulch will add valuable organic material to the soil. Raised beds to the rear (which allow the soil to warm up more quickly for early spring plantings) contain hearty lettuce, carrots, young beet, and heavily mulched sweetcorn, tomatoes and celery.

8. Care of the soil. A well fed, well conditioned soil grows strong healthy plants, i.e., understanding that the welfare of our plants is in direct proportion to the health of the soil in which we place them.
9. The practice of crop rotation. Planting crops on a rotation system avoids a build-up of plant-specific diseases in the soil and prevents the same nutrients being continuously extracted until crops fail.

Crop rotation

The traditional way of ensuring that every plant has the minerals and nutrients it requires is by planting it in a section of the potager devoted to plants with similar needs. These sections are rotated around the garden year by year on a three or four year cycle, giving the system its name of 'crop rotation'. The system ensures that repeated crops of one variety do not take out the same minerals and nutrients from the soil each year, so that eventually the crop starves and fails.

Crop rotation is also immensely important because some plants actually put minerals or nitrogen into the ground as they grow. Crop rotation need not cramp your style. You may think it difficult to achieve the colour schemes and plant contrasts you desire if all you can grow in one bed are members of the cabbage family, but as we have seen, a huge variety of brassicas may be grown together – wine-red and silver-blue cabbages, pale green or dark green, smooth skinned or crinkly skinned, and then there are all those marvellous oriental varieties which don't look like cabbages at all! Practising crop rotation also helps the organic gardener reduce the pest and disease concentration. Growing the same plants in the same soil each year encourages a build-up of insects, viruses and disease spores which afflict one type of vegetable, so the more often crops are rotated the healthier both the vegetables and soil will be.

Crop rotation plan
Year 1
Bed 1: Grow root crops (salsify, parsnips, carrots, beetroot). Do not add lime or manure this area.
Bed 2: Sow potatoes. Add plentiful manure but no lime.
Bed 3: Grow other crops (celery, onions, peas, cucumber, pumpkins, sweetcorn, salad crops). Check soil acidity and add lime if necessary. Manure well.
Bed 4: Plant brassicas (cabbages, broccoli, kales, Brussels sprouts, cauliflowers, radish, turnips, kohlrabi). Dress with lime but only add manure if soil is short of organic matter.

Year 2
Bed 1: sow potatoes.
Bed 2: grow other crops.
Bed 3: grow brassicas.
Bed 4: root crops.

Year 3
Bed 1: grow other crops.
Bed 2: plant brassicas.
Bed 3: root crops.
Bed 4: grow potatoes.

Year 4
Bed 1: grow brassicas.
Bed 2: grow roots.
Bed 3: grow potatoes.
Bed 4: grow other crops.

Year 5: as year one.

In the potager, especially where there are multiple beds, these divisions need not be followed rigidly as long as the crops are rotated over at least three years. The general rule is that the longer before any crop is growing in the same place, the better.

Insects and biological control
Beneficial insects exert natural control in the garden by eating those that are pests. If the former are eliminated by non-specific pesticides, or by organic preparations used at incorrect strength, any pests which survive will flourish. Their natural predators destroyed, they breed unchecked and one becomes locked in an unrelenting cycle of synthetic chemical control. Similarly, if total annihilation of bad insects takes place, beneficial insects which have survived will starve, which in turn leads to a poor pollination rate and low fertility throughout the garden. The aim is to maintain a happy balance by using the correct spray at correct strength, at the correct time, and *only* on those areas in which an unacceptable level of undesirable insect infestation or disease may be *seen*.

The organic gardener has a different perception of the old adage 'prevention is better than cure'; he or she does not spray the entire garden, but works instead towards a 'live and let live' philosophy, that is, the *balance* of good and bad insects existing for mutual benefit, which is what nature intended before man destroyed that balance.

Plant hosts for beneficial insects
The bug-eat-bug approach encourages the provision of host plants for both types of insects. The organic gardener backs up his or her spray programme with companion planting; that is, with combinations of herbs and other plants which will attract or repel insects as required. Specific varieties are used as host plants on which beneficial insects may feed and breed. One of the most valuable of these is *Phacelia tanacetifolia* which is used extensively in horticulture and agriculture for the control of white butterfly and aphid pests.

Phacelia is a beautiful plant which grows to 45 cm (18 in). It has filmy foliage and fluffy blue flowerheads freely borne over an extended period. It attracts that most voracious of predators, the hoverfly. The adult female hoverfly needs to eat pollen to bring her eggs to maturity and be assured of colonies of aphids on which to feed the larvae. The hoverfly resembles a honey bee in shape, but displays brilliant metallic colours. Adult flies have a short tongue so in addition to phacelia, which is their favourite food, it is best to arrange other suitable plantings such as marigolds, poached-egg flower (*Limnanthes douglasii*), and baby blue-eyes (*Nemophilia insignis*). Hoverflies will also eat aphids, scale insects, small caterpillars and caterpillar eggs – which makes them deserving of bed and breakfast in any garden!

Phacelia also attracts other predatory insects such as lacewings and ladybirds. The lacewing *Micromus tasmaniae* preys on aphids, mealy bugs, thrips, scale insects, moth eggs and mites, including those of the red spider.

Ladybirds are a most precious garden resident. They are reputed to each eat at least 100 aphids a day and also relish scale insects, mealy bugs, leaf hoppers, whitefly, mites, the potato beetle and the bean beetle. Aphids are so predominant because there is a world shortage of ladybirds, due to massive global usage of DDT in the '60s and '70s. Horticultural scientists say their numbers are increasing only slowly.

The food fetish of that other most beneficial insect, the praying mantis, includes caterpillars, aphids and leaf hoppers.

Companion planting – employing flowers and herbs for pest control

All strongly scented culinary herbs can be used as 'pest confusers', either by planting them close to the 'victim' plants, by cutting their leaves to mulch tender new transplants, or by steeping them in water to make organic insecticides. A handful of the leaves of feverfew (*Chrysanthemum parthenium*) spread around transplanted seedlings is an excellent insect-repelling mulch.

One of the best known flowers for pest control is the French marigold, which is not edible. It is employed to repel aphids, cabbage-white butterflies above the ground, and nematodes underground. The dwarf cultivars *Tagetes tenuifolia* are said to ward off nematodes and to stimulate the growth of beans, cucumber, aubergines/eggplants, melons, potatoes, pumpkins and tomatoes. They look wonderful under sweetcorn and tomatoes and make excellent temporary edgings or 'fast fillers' in awkward corners.

Other flower species extensively used as companion plants of great benefit in the potager are *Calendula officinalis* (pot marigold), borage (*Borago officinalis*), and nasturtiums (*Tropaeolum majus*). In addition to being aesthetically pleasing, their pungent perfumes stimulate plant growth, and in the case of calendula and tagetes, deter nematodes in the soil. Calendula is also credited with deterring beetles among asparagus and working against nematodes among carrots, tomatoes and beetroot.

Artemisia: though on the large side, artemisias have beautiful silver feathery foliage and pungent scents which are said to repel flies and other insect pests from vegetables planted nearby. Wormwood (*Artemisia absinthium*), height 1.5 m (5 ft), makes a most attractive shrub – cut it back at least twice a year to keep it compact. It provides an eyecatching combination when coupled with the pink flowers of marjoram. Southernwood (*A. abrotanum*) reaches about the same size and is a vigorous spreader. *A. schmidtiana* rarely exceeds a growth habit of 60 cm (2 ft) in height and width. The artemisia family is drought tolerant and hardy in all but poorly drained soils.

Borage (*Borago officinalis*) is said to improve the flavour of cucurbits and tomatoes, increase the disease resistance of strawberries, and to protect cabbage and kale plants from pests such as stink bugs and flea beetles. The plant also serves as an attractant for aphids, which might at first seem like an excellent idea for not growing it, but see how you feel when the borage next to your dwarf beans is liberally adorned with the pest while your beans remain totally unscathed! Since borage self sows readily, remove the pest-infested plants and burn them as soon as new seedlings appear.

Attractive companion plantings of French marigolds, dwarf feverfew and calendula protect lettuce, tomatoes, onions, beet and other vegetables from insect pests.

Chervil (*Anthriscus cerefolium*), growing to 25–50 cm (9–20 in), is believed to protect lettuce against aphids, mildew, snails and slugs and also to keep away ants.

Chives (*Allium schoenoprasum*), hardy herbs growing to 30 cm (1 ft), are believed to be particularly beneficial as companion plants to roses, helping prevent black spot and mildew, and deter aphids and other pests.

Dill (*Antheum graveolens*), an annual growing to 90 cm (3 ft), is said to deter carrot fly, slugs and snails. Self sows.

Garlic (*Allium sativum*) and other members of the onion family have been valued since ancient times for their insect-repellent properties. For example, garlic makes an ideal edging for a bed of parsnips or carrots in the potager and as underplanting beneath roses in the flower garden. This herb is now used extensively for the manufacture of organic insect-repellent sprays.

Nasturtiums (*Tropaeolum majus*) are useful in both dwarf and climbing varieties. Set among cabbage-family plants, celery and cucumbers, these are said to deter beetles and aphids and to improve the flavour of cucumber, radishes and courgettes/zucchini. Some gardeners say that while nasturtiums repel woolly aphids, they attract the black variety, but others consider this a good reason for planting the flower because it acts as a decoy plant. Lateral thinking – as with borage, better to have legions of the black pest on the nasturtiums than on the cabbages.

Other plants we may employ in our gardens to promote biological pest control would include brassicas, which are left to flower, parsnips, carrots, parsley, angelica, fennel, thyme and coriander. Also attractive to predatory beneficial insects are bergamot, mints, spearmint, yarrow, artemisias, cosmos, Michaelmas daisies and other daisy species. Insect-repelling plants include tansy, mint, pennyroyal, garlic, chives and wormwood. Basil is truly the gardener's friend (especially in the greenhouse) – bees love it, aphids, fruitfly, whitefly and the housefly loathe it.

It is argued that natural control methods used by organic gardeners are not always as effective as more orthodox treatments. It is true that environmentally friendly plant derivative sprays (with the exception of Neemseed oil, which is discussed later) are non-systemic, that is, they do not, as with toxic chemicals, enter the system of the plant and afford continued protection. Plant-derivative sprays fall into two categories, pesticides and anti-feedants. The pesticides kill the pest while the anti-feedant repels and acts as a prevention to pest infestation.

A certain level of pests and disease will remain because organic preparations kill or deter only when they come in contact with the bodies of the insects they are designed to deal with. Thus they need to be used more frequently and it is essential that all parts of the plants, including the undersides of the leaves, are thoroughly covered.

It is possible to minimise even the use of organic sprays by utilising the time that would be spent spraying inspecting one's vegetables regularly. Brassicas, for example, are prey to infestations of caterpillars at certain times of the year. Turn a few leaves as often as you can and rub out the pests and their colonies of egg clusters (green thumb!).

There is no doubt that initially 'going organic' takes courage and more than a few dark nights of the soul after the whole garden seems to be chewed, razored, pock-marked or skeletal. Be assured that your garden, the birds and the bees will live to tell the tale, thriving as beneficial insects and pestiferous varieties find a natural balance. By employing the alternative methods outlined in this chapter, the feared horticultural decimation of biblical proportions from plagues of gruesome insects will not eventuate!

Green manures

This is a method of improving the fertility and moisture retention of the soil by growing crops especially to dig in. Green manures and mulches are of value to the vegetable garden in several ways, including that of decorative effect. It is better to see a bed covered and protected by a green manure crop such as blue-flowered lupins or phacelia while not in use, than bare and covered with weeds. The practical benefits of using green manures include: employing plants' strong roots to break up the soil; some add nitrogen, or draw out minerals which are thus made available for following crops; they grow quickly and suppress weeds; some, such as rye, cleanse the soil; cut and allowed to dry, green manures produce a thick mass of beneficial mulch or compost.

Green manure plants

Mustard: common mustard is valued because it is hardy, grows fast as a filler or cover plant (three weeks), has bright green cheerful foliage and yellow or white flowers if allowed to grow on. When cut or dug in it decomposes quickly. Mustard is recommended as underplanting for tomatoes and is said to disinfect the soil, but in this position it must be trimmed back to a foot high.

Lupins: the ordinary blue-flowered variety which matures quickly is the most commonly used. Seeds are readily available from any garden centre.

Phacelia: Probably the best green manure of all, and the most decorative, is phacelia or 'bee's friend'. There are two popular varieties, *P. tanacetifolia* and *P. campanularia*, the former has soft violet-blue feathery flowers, and the latter dark blue bells. A legume with very special qualities as a host plant for hoverflies (see page 109), phacelia also enriches the soil with nitrogen, and is not only a quick filler but a beautiful flowering plant in bloom over a long season.

Healthy new season's vegetables emerge from well composted raised beds and young seedlings are warmed and protected from the birds with a mesh frame. Plantings of chives and calendula help to repel chewing pests and borders of lobelia flowers attract bees and beneficial insects.

Making compost

Bulky organic matter is the very basis of fertility in the ornamental kitchen garden and home-made garden compost should make up a large part of it. It is a soil conditioner second to none, improving both drainage and moisture-retaining capacity, and provides a home for millions of beneficial micro-organisms and plant food.

The best method of composting is known as the aerobic method, which will produce usable compost in just over three months. You will require a robust bin such as the black polythene composters readily available in garden centres. They are bottomless and have holes in their sides for ventilation, but their one disadvantage is that although they have a lid, it is difficult to fork and turn the compost while it is maturing. When the material is ready for use, the entire shell of the bin is lifted up, leaving a neat cone-shaped pile. Alternatively one can construct a compost container of wooden slats, bricks or netting, which allows air to circulate but is enclosed enough to encourage the heat to build up within the organic materials.

If possible, it is best to build two bins side by

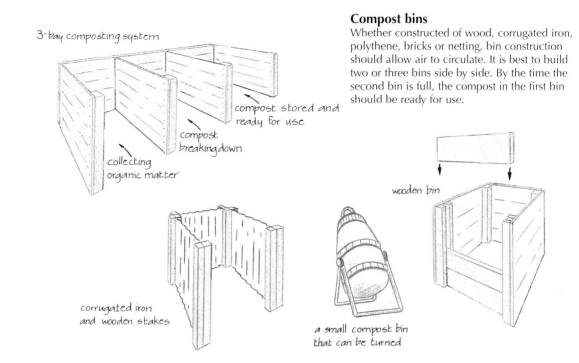

3-bay composting system

compost stored and ready for use

compost breaking down

collecting organic matter

corrugated iron and wooden stakes

wooden bin

a small compost bin that can be turned

Compost bins

Whether constructed of wood, corrugated iron, polythene, bricks or netting, bin construction should allow air to circulate. It is best to build two or three bins side by side. By the time the second bin is full, the compost in the first bin should be ready for use.

side, so that by the time the second bin is full the compost in the first should be ready for use. This way one always has some of this organic staff-of-life compost to hand.

When you have accumulated enough material to start the bin, pierce the soil beneath with a fork to allow excess water to drain away and encourage the earthworms to enter and start work upon the organic materials. Mix the materials well and put them into the container in layers about 30 cm (1 ft) thick with a sprinkling of activator between layers. This can be a proprietary product, ammonium sulphate or animal manure.

When the bin is full, cover it with a piece of old carpet or punctured polythene and leave it to heat up. The heating process, which will take about a month, is important to ensure that the seeds of weeds and any pathogens are destroyed. At this stage the compost should be turned and re-covered. The process will need to be repeated once more before the compost is properly mature – the finest, crumbliest, sweetest-smelling soil conditioner imaginable!

Mulches

Mulches are invaluable for helping to retain moisture in the soil by preventing evaporation and, if they contain plenty of organic materials, they will also feed and condition the soil and help produce bumper crops. However, gardeners have divided opinions about mulch in the potager where aesthetics are of prime consideration. The truth is that any mulch which does not consist of equal-sized pieces does look messy, and layers of old pea straw get scratched up by the birds and can blow about. Mulches made of bark are not suitable for the potager, which takes us right back to the compost bin.

Try to have a light covering of compost and well-rotted manure covering the soil at all times; this feeds the plants as well as keeping roots moist. Mulches of green-manure crops grown as part of the crop rotation plan are excellent since they are cut down and dug in at maturity and decompose quickly.

Watering

No matter how well you mulch or compost, there are times when the vegetable garden has to be watered. Your homegrown produce, although full of health and organically grown, will not be cost effective if you must stand for hours with a hose in your hand. Garden centres offer a wide range of relatively inexpensive DIY irrigation and sprinkler systems which will efficiently water all parts of the potager when required.

Non-toxic sprays, fungicides and insecticides

In addition to their value as insect-repellents or attractants, some flowering plants are useful for preparing non-toxic insecticides and these are also cultivated by organic gardeners. They include garlic, rhubarb, pyrethrum and artemisias.

It is absolutely essential that organic sprays be used at the recommended strengths. It is a temptation to make them stronger where infestations of pests and disease are severe, but it is more important to remember that, used in excess, they can be as lethal as non-organic preparations, both to insects good and bad, and to the very plants you are trying to protect!

Organic products, commercial and homemade

Although most garden centres now offer a small range of non-toxic preparations, it is neither difficult nor expensive to make one's own organic pesticides and herbicides. However, some products are so long-lasting it is hardly worth the effort involved in making them yourself, e.g., the following concentrate.

Garlic and pyrethrum concentrate

This preparation is widely available from most nurseries and garden centres. The garlic content is a pest repellent, and the pyrethrum flower extract an organic insecticide, but please note that it is toxic to bees. Spraying should not therefore take place until just after sundown when they have stopped working the flowers. The rate at which this preparation should be applied is at a dilution of approximately 20–25 ml (1–1$\frac{1}{2}$ tablespoons) to 1 litre (2 pints) of water. Compatibility: do *not* use with lime sulphur, Bordeaux mix or other alkaline preparations.

It is possible to make your own garlic and pyrethrum sprays if you wish, but I have found a 200 ml (7$\frac{1}{2}$ oz) bottle of this commercially prepared concentrate lasts for six months or more for spot spraying in a large garden.

Garlic spray (repellent)

Method: Chop 6 large cloves of garlic and place in a blender with 6 tablespoons of medicinal paraffin oil and pulverise. Leave the pulp to stand for 48 hours. Grate 1 tablespoon of oil-based soap into a container and add 500 ml (1 pint) of hot water, stirring until the soap has melted. Stir into the garlic pulp. When cool, strain into jars, label clearly and store in the fridge. When spraying, use 2 tablespoons garlic mixture to 1 litre (2 pints) of water.

Pyrethrum insecticide spray

The silver-leafed pyrethrum daisy (*Chrysanthemum cinerariifolium*) contains substances called pyrethrins which act directly on the nervous systems of insects such as aphids, mites and caterpillars – and bees, so remember the spray after sundown rule.

Method: Take 1 tablespoon of well crushed flowers of the silver-leafed pyrethrum daisy, *Chrysanthemum cinerariifolium* (syn. *Pyrethrum cinerariifolium*) and mix with sufficient spirit alcohol to wet the flowers and release the pyrethrin extracts. (The flowers may be harvested, dried and stored for use at other times of the year.) Place the crushed mixture into 2 litres (4 pints) of hot water and add a squirt of soft or natural soap (not detergent) to aid the spray's stickability. Allow to stand and strain into airtight jars when cool. *Label clearly* and store in fridge.

Dozing on duty, the sleepy scarecrow needs the help of companion plants to protect organically grown crops. Blue flowered *Phacelia tanacetifolia* (front left) is an important host plant for beneficial insects that prey on insect pests. Borders of chives around the old pink rose act as repellent plants. Intensive vegetable production in a small area such as this is helped by well-conditioned and humus-enriched soil.

Neemseed oil insecticide

Oil from the neem tree (*Azadirachta indica*) is the only botanical systemic organic pesticide yet available, and it is highly efficient for controlling a large variety of plant-feeding and sucking pests, including whitefly, scale, mealybug, thrips and nematodes. Neemseed oil products are an environmentally benign form of pest control for use in horticulture, agriculture, on flowers and turf.

Azadirachtin, the main ingredient of neemseed oil, has proven harmless to beneficial insects and predators. It has been used for centuries in India as a food preservative and to prevent insects eating stored grain. A systemic, it repels and deters leaf-eating and plant-sucking insects by suppressing their appetite and affecting bowel activity.

Applied at the early stages of insect growth, it can influence the development of eggs, larvae and pupae. At the larvae and nymph stage, neemseed oil disrupts the metamorphosis process.

Neemseed oil may be used after diluting with lukewarm water at a ratio of 1:200, or 0.5%, e.g., 1 litre of neem 1% with 200 litres of water or 0.5 litres of neem 1% with 100 litres of water. Solutions for spraying should be prepared by stirring neemseed oil into the appropriate amount of water. Use the solution as soon as possible and spray the affected plants until they are dripping wet. The mix should not be stored longer than about two days under normal room conditions.

If you do not wish to purchase commercially prepared neem, an effective insecticide may be made with a cake of neem soap from a Trade Aid shop.

To make neem spray: You will need a grater, a cake of neem soap, a 5-litre bucket, a whisk and a sieve, storage jars or bottles (and a strong arm).

Method: Grate a quarter of a cake of neem into the bucket, pour on about a litre (2 pints) of boiling water to make a liquid, stir thoroughly to dissolve lumps, then add 4 more litres (8 pints) of water. Strain the liquid into bottles or jars. Label clearly and store in a cool place. (For dilution rates see the preceding page.)

Organic spray for black spot and downy mildew

Particularly effective on roses and cucurbits.

Method: Take 1 teaspoon of baking soda, 1 teaspoon of cocide oil (a vegetable oil) and mix with 1 litre (2 pints) of water. Spray every 10 days for continued protection against black spot and mildew.

Rhubarb spray

The leaves of the homely rhubarb, boiled, also make a useful insecticide.

Method: Boil 1 kg (2 lb) of leaves in 2 litres (4 pints) of water for 30 minutes – *do not use an aluminium saucepan*. When cool, remove the leaves, strain the fluid and mix with enough pure soap to make it frothy. *Label clearly* and store in a cool dark place.

Wormwood infusion

A strong infusion of bitter smelling and tasting wormwood (*Artemisia absinthium*) over and around the base of young plants is an excellent slug and snail repellent – but like all organic infusions it needs to be applied regularly to be effective. Since this mix does not need straining, I keep a bucket filled with steeping leaves and pour it out, leaves and all, wherever gastropods have become a nuisance.

Efficient homemade sprays cost little to make and may be made in larger quantities to save time. When the mixtures are cool and strained, bottle, *label clearly* and store in a cool, dark place.

Organic fungicides

Copper oxychloride preparations ('Super Copper DF' ('Kocide df') active ingredient 400 kg/copper as cupric hydroxide) are available at all garden centres in the form of a wettable powder which controls fungal and bacterial diseases such as blight, downy mildew, black spot, leaf curl and shothole. The general application rate for roses and ornamentals is approximately 7.5 g to 5 litres of water ($^1/_4$ oz to 10 pints), and specific rates for individual fruit and vegetables are clearly stated on the pack. Pour the powder into water slowly, stirring well. There are a number of similar copper oxychloride preparations on the market. All are non-systemic, i.e., they are not absorbed into the system of the plant and unlike toxic sprays do not therefore give continued protection. Regular applications and full plant coverage is essential. Try to cover the underside of the leaves as thoroughly as the topside.

Conqueror spraying oil, cocide, all-purpose oil and others

These non-toxic mineral or vegetable oils control scale, mites and mealybug on a wide range of ornamentals, fruit and vegetables. They are compatible with copper oxychloride fungicide preparations and are generally used together as an organic insecticide and fungicide. The combination is popular as a general 'clean-up' spray before and after pruning and during winter. The oils are for use in both winter and early summer.

Several organic insecticides widely available for the control of aphids, greenfly, mealy bugs, mites, thrips and whitefly on roses, vegetables and ornamentals contain biodegradable fatty acids and potassium salts in the form of a soluble concentrate. The same ingredients combined at a far more concentrated strength are employed

Opposite: The flower heads of *Achillea* 'Salmon Beauty' attract beneficial predatory insects and aromatic golden feverfew (lower right) repels insect pests. The unusual climbing bean on the tepee (rear) is the purple-flowered, foliaged and podded 'Violetta Cornetti', whose blooms are highly attractive to bees.

as an organic herbicide. In this preparation the same fatty acids are so highly concentrated that they work by destroying cells in the tissues of undesirable plants. The use of the fatty acids and potassium salts at different strengths for *both protection and destruction* of plant material heavily underlines how vital it is to use *exactly* the strength recommended by the manufacturer.

Barriers and other organic plant protection methods

Trees, particularly fruiting varieties, can be protected against flightless insects with sticky bands and collars. These trap the larvae as they crawl up the trunk from the ground. The band should be thickly coated with vaseline, engine grease or any sticky non-toxic material of this nature.

Pests and diseases on trees are also controlled by frequent applications of the organic sprays already discussed, using a slightly stronger concentration. The copper and mineral oil preparations discussed opposite are particularly good for prevention and treatment of brown rot and leaf curl on peach, plum and nectarine trees.

Slug and snail deterrents

Non-toxic products to deter slugs and snails are composed mainly of a coarse gritty powder which works on a barrier principle, like crushed eggshells. Alternatively, you can ring tender seedlings with a barrier of coarse sand. The

'jaws' of the gastropod world will not cross sharp or gritty substances. To give maximum results, these materials need to be applied regularly, particularly after rain. This involves a little more work, which is acceptable because toxic slug pellets can poison children, birds, family pets and hedgehogs. Clear plastic bottles with the bottoms cut out also form excellent protection and insulation for young plants.

The organic formula

My homemade 'three-in-one' repellent, insecticide and fungicide consists of:
1. Garlic: insect deterrent.
2. Pyrethrum: organic insecticide.
3. Copper oxychloride: preventative and protection against fungal and bacterial diseases.

These three preparations are all compatible and combine to promote plant health. They offer protection to edibles, roses and ornamentals against insect pests, fungal and bacterial diseases. The dilution rates for commercial preparations are clearly stated on the packets, and those for the homemade sprays have been detailed in the recipes.

If, like me, you are a 'rosophile' and enjoy these flowers in the potager as well as in the main gardens, accept that where there are roses, there is black spot and downy mildews. Even when the plants are drenched with toxic chemicals, these disfiguring diseases remain to some extent.

The purpose of organic gardening is to strengthen the plants' resistance to diseases and pests without the use of unnatural agencies. The soil is a living organism and remains healthy if it is used and fertilised biologically. Consider the thought that 'bios' is Greek for life; biology is the science of life; biological means according to the laws of life.

Screw up your courage, go forth and plant your potager for the new season, and phase out those prettily packaged poisons.

BIBLIOGRAPHY

Art of French Vegetable Gardening, Louisa Jones, Artisan Publishing, 1995.

Kings Seed Catalogue Australia and New Zealand, 1996/7, Kings Herbs, 1996.

The Complete New Zealand Gardener, Geoff Bryant and Eion Scarrow, David Bateman Ltd, 1995.

The Herb Garden Displayed, Gilian Painter and Elaine Power, Hodder & Stoughton, 1979.

The Ornamental Kitchen Garden, Janet MacDonald, David and Charles, 1994. (Extract used by kind permission of the publishers.)

The Traditional Garden, Graham Rose, Dorling Kindersley, 1989.

ACKNOWLEDGEMENTS

The author, photographer and publisher would like to thank:

'Barewood', Caroline and Joe Ferraby, pages 24, 25, 28, 33t, 33b, 41, 72, 74

'Barnsley House', Rosemary Verey, Cirencester, Gloucestershire, pages 1, 16t, 23, 37b, 46–7, 53, 55, 61, 68–9, 89

'Bellevue', Vivian Papich, pages 5, 91, 92c

'Bourton House', Bourton-on-Mill, Gloucestershire, pages 12–13, 42, 50b

'Brown Sugar Cafe', page 97

Liza Caughey, page 49t

Phil Cooke, pages 17, 18, 99

Christine and Phillip Crawshaw, pages 7, 36tl

'Denmans', John Brookes, page 82

Olive Dunn, pages 54, 86–7

Julia and Andrew Everist, pages 57, 77

Julie Fulton, pages 15b, 36tc

Rodney Fumpston, pages 52, 84–5, 117

'Gethsemane', Bev and Ken Loader, page 35b

Kay Green, pages 10, 12

'Hadspen Garden and Nursery', N. & S. Pope, Castle Cary, Somerset, page 73

Annie Heywood, back cover, page 95

'Kiri Kiri Gardens', Robyn and Joe Woollaston, page 37tr

'Koanga Nurseries', Kay Baxter, page 108

Jim and Pat Lawson, page 98

'Le Potager', Joanna Stewart, pages 16b, 71, 81

Richard Luisetti, page 83

Nancy McCabe, Falls Village, Connecticut, pages 43, 93

Liz Mackmurdie, front cover, pages 15t, 29, 35tl, 44t, 88, 90, 92b, 110

'The Master's Garden', Lord Leycester Hospital, Warwickshire, pages 30, 34t, 40t, 45

'The Millton Vineyard', page 48

'Moss Green Gardens', Jo and Bob Munro, pages 35tr, 47r, 112

Ann Norris, page 27

'Nymet', Jean and Colin Sanders, page 44b

'Ohinetahi', Sir Miles Warren, page 26

'The Old Rectory', Mr and Mrs Anthony Huntington, Sudsborough, Kettering, pages 6, 11, 49b, 50–1

Helen Phare, page 96

'Rathmoy', Suzanne Grace, page 38b

'Rosemoor Gardens', RHS, Great Torrington, Devon, pages 39, 75

Clare and Alex Scott, pages 31, 40b

'Shackleton Gardens', Clonsilla, Dublin, page 65

Robyn Sygrove, page 92t

'Taipari Point', Annette Johnston, page 38t

'Valley Homestead', Diana and Brian Anthony, pages 2, 14, 34b, 115

INDEX